# Steam in Action
# 'CASTLES'

# Steam in Action

# 'CASTLES'

## Laurence Waters

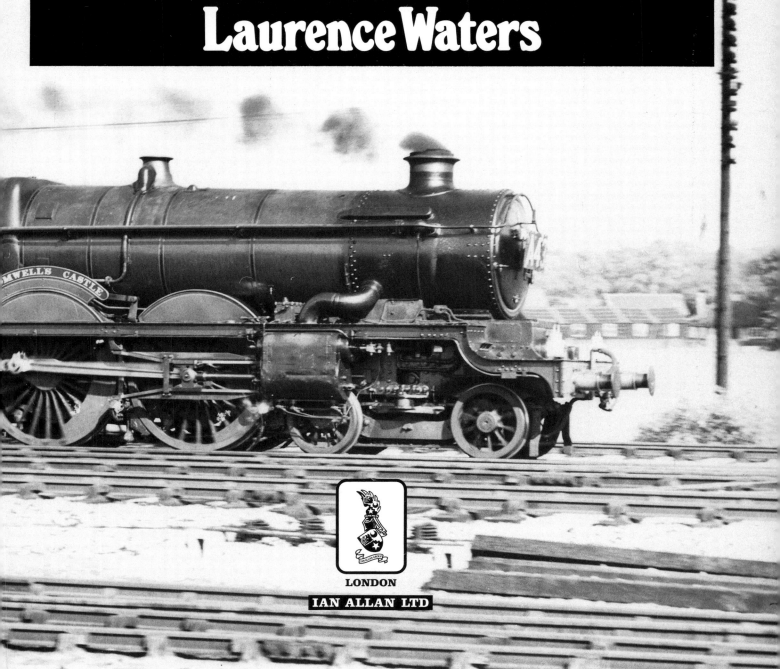

LONDON

IAN ALLAN LTD

First published 1991

ISBN 0 7110 2006 X

Published by Ian Allan Ltd, Shepperton, Surrey; and printed by Ian Allan Printing Ltd at their works at Coombelands in Runnymede, England

## Acknowledgements

I would like to thank the following individuals and associations for their help in producing this book: A. E. Doyle, J. D. Edwards, G. F. Heiron, S. Boorne, D. Tuck, Dr G. Smith, G. Hine, P. Q. Treloar, P. Kelley, D. Sellman, M. Mensing, C. R. L. Coles, the Ian Allan Library, the Great Western Society, the Oxford University Railway Society and the Great Western Trust.

# Contents

*Front cover:*
**The down 'Cathedrals Express', the 5.15pm ex-Paddington, passes Iver, Bucks on 25 August 1962 hauled by No 7007 *Great Western*. *Peter Fry/Great Western Trust.***

*Back cover:*
**No 5054 *Earl of Ducie* prepares to leave Paddington on 16 May 1964 with the Oxford University Railway Society 'Castle Farewell' tour. *D. Tuck***

*Half title:*
**No 5081 *Lockheed Hudson* leaves Reading with a down West of England train Note the one white/one red headcode lamps. *M. W. Earley***

*Previous page:*
**No 7031 *Cromwell's Castle* passing Didcot with an Oxford-Paddington express during the summer of 1962. *David A. Anderson***

*Right:*
**No 5089 *Westminster Abbey* ascending Patchway Bank, Bristol. *R. O. Coffin***

# Introduction

I suppose that it is every author's dream to be able to produce a book about his favourite class of steam locomotive. In doing so I have been fortunate in being allowed access to the archives of the Great Western Trust collection at Didcot, from where much of the background material has been found. The Great Western Society has also kindly allowed me to use *Great Western Echo* articles written some 27 years ago by the late Jack Hancock, regarding the Ian Allan high speed runs of 1964. This, together with many previously unpublished photographs of the class in action during the 1950s and 1960s and a cross-section of 'Castle' allocations taken from the official registers at Kew will, I hope, add something to the working knowledge of these remarkable locomotives.

*Below:*
**No 5061** *Earl of Birkenhead* **(with tall chimney) approaches Harbury cement works with a down Birmingham via Oxford service on 13 March 1957.** *J. D. Edwards*

# Chapter One

## THE EVOLUTION OF THE 'CASTLES'

It is now some 26 years since the last examples of the 'Castle' class were withdrawn from BR service. What was and still is, the attraction? The reason perhaps is that during their 40 years of main line operation, the 'Castles' gained a reputation for fine performance, free running and excellent economy, which together with their undoubted good looks represented all that was best in not only Great Western, but British locomotive design. In order to trace the evolution of the 'Castles' we have to go back to around the turn of the century, when express passenger engines on the Great Western Railway consisted mainly of 4-4-0 designs such as the 'Atbara', 'Bulldog', 'Duke', 'Badminton', 'City' and 'County' classes. Good though these locomotives were, they were really too small for the heavier trains required by the operating department.

When the first 'Castle' was built in 1923, its design had evolved from development work started by Churchward some 20 years earlier, and continued by Collett in replacing the 4-4-0s with a new and more powerful class of express passenger locomotive. To this

end a prototype two-cylinder 4-6-0, No 100, was constructed at Swindon in February 1902, and a year later two further 'experimental' locomotives, Nos 98 and 171 *Albion*, both two-cylinder 4-6-0s, entered traffic. Nos 98 and 100 ran with boiler pressures of 200lb/sq in, whereas a higher boiler pressure of 225lb/sq in was used on No 171.

At this time the Nord Railway in France was successfully using De Glehn, four-cylinder compound Atlantics on some of their faster services such as the Paris-Calais boat trains. It was generally acknowledged that at that time the De Glehns were the finest class of passenger locomotives in Europe. Churchward was naturally interested in the possibility of incorporating some of the features of the French locomotives in his own designs. In order to effect a comparison between his own prototypes, which were still very much in the development stage, and the French locomotives, he persuaded the Great Western to purchase at a cost of about £4,000 a De Glehn Atlantic from the Societe Alsacienne de Constructions Mechanique of Belfort. The new locomotive was

placed into Great Western stock during October 1903, and numbered 102. In 1905 two further French Atlantics were purchased, being numbered 103 and 104. All three were subsequently named: No 102 became *La France*, 103 *President* and 104 *Alliance*.

In order to gain an even better comparison between the French locomotives and his own, No 171 was converted into an Atlantic during October 1904. Obviously Churchward was still undecided about his final design, for in June 1906 Swindon constructed yet another Atlantic, numbered 40: it was named *North Star*. However unlike No 171 this locomotive was provided with four simple expansion cylinders, a scissors valve gear, and a boiler pressure of 225lb/sq in.

Eventually the comparisons and trials between the various locomotives led Churchward to the conclusion that with its greater adhesion and lower running costs, a 4-6-0 six-coupled

*Below:*
**De Glehn compound No 104 *Alliance* stands at Leamington with an up service to Oxford, c1923. *Author's Collection***

*Above:*
**The 8.50am service from Birkenhead arrives at Paddington on 27 August 1910 hauled by De Glehn Compound No 102 *La France*. *LCGB Ken Nunn Collection***

arrangement would be more suitable for Great Western use. The compound principle was also abandoned in favour of the simple expansion layout used on No 40. In 1907 No 4001 *Dog Star*, the first of the new 'Star' class 4-6-0s rolled out of Swindon. The scissors valve gear fitted to No 40 was dropped for the production 'Stars' in favour of a specially designed Walschaert valve gear. There is some doubt as to exactly why this decision was made by Churchward but J. C. Gibson who once worked with the valve setting gang in A shop produced an interesting article in the *Great Western Echo* some years ago which offered a possible explanation. It appears that it was extremely difficult to set up the scissors gear on No 40. The task apparently often took from 10 to 14 days to get right, as opposed to a day and a half for other types, and although this time could have been tolerated for a single locomotive it would have proved impossibly time consuming for a class that eventually totalled 73. No 40 *North Star* was eventually rebuilt as a 4-6-0 during 1909, and in 1912 it was renumbered 4000.

Including the *North Star* prototype, there were some 61 'Stars' constructed between 1907 and 1914. This number was supplemented by a further 12 which were completed by Collett dur-

ing 1922/23. The 'Stars' proved to be very able locomotives and were used by the Great Western on most of its principal services. The end of World War I saw Great Western passenger services restored back to prewar levels. Together with the steady growth in passenger traffic, this once again saw the requirement for more powerful locomotives. Certainly prior to his retirement in December 1921, Churchward had in his mind the idea of producing a larger 'Star', incorporating the No 7 boiler that he had successfully used on the '4700' class mixed traffic '2-8-0's. Although the idea was a good one, the combination would have taken the axle loading above the 20 ton limit set by the civil engineers at the time, and this would have restricted the use of these 'Super Stars' over many routes.

Collett took over the post of Chief Mechanical Engineer from Churchward on 1 January 1922. Rather surprisingly there had been little in the way of new designs produced by the company for quite a number of years, so one of Collett's first tasks was to continue Churchward's work on producing a new express type. The directive from the management indicated that the new locomotives should both supplement and replace the 'Stars' on the heavier loadings now being demanded, whilst remaining within the 20 ton axle loading.

Collett's answer to this problem was very similar to Churchward's in that he took the basic 'Star' layout and improved it by fitting a new larger but

lighter (No 8) boiler. The result became the 'Castle' class.

Although the new class had several up to date features, they also made use of many established standard parts and were to all intents and purposes just an enlarged 'Star'. The general layout of the frames and wheel spacing were the same as the 'Stars', but the cylinders were of an increased diameter of 16in as opposed to the 15in of the 'Stars'. The new No 8 boiler was 3in larger in diameter than the old No 1, the firebox was lengthened to give an increased grate area of some 30sq ft and tractive effort was increased from 27,800lb to 31,625lb. One of the chief features of the new design was the enlarged side windowed cab, which not only gave a more balanced look to the locomotives but provided a vast improvement in accommodation for the crew. It is probably true to say that the whole 'Castle' design was a bit of a compromise, in order to keep the locomotive within the 20 ton axle limit. The axle loading on the new locomotives was actually only 19.5 tons. However, whether by chance or design, the combination of the new boiler, the outside curved steam pipes, and the larger cab gave the 'Castles' a well proportioned look that was to make them immediately attractive to both officials and public alike.

The first 'Castle', No 4073 *Caerphilly Castle*, appeared in August 1923, and was turned out with full lining, brass beading and a copper capped chimney. It must have looked tremendous and probably signalled the end of the post-

No 4074 *Caldicot Castle* showed a coal consumption of only 2.83lb/drawbar horsepower, a quite remarkable figure as the norm at the time was between 4 and 5lb. The excellent boiler was evaporating approximately one gallon of water for each pound of coal used. Under general operating conditions Castles were showing a saving in coal consumption over the 'Star' class of some 6 to 7%.

The construction of the new locomotives saw the Great Western publicity machine go into full swing. *Caerphilly Castle* was displayed at the Empire Exhibition at Wembley in 1924 with the GWR proudly announcing that their new 'Castle' engines were the most powerful steam locomotives in the country at that time. Taken with a pinch of salt by the other companies, subsequent trials were to prove the statement to be true. On 28 April 1924 King George V and Queen Mary visited Swindon works, the Royal train being hauled to Swindon by No 4082 *Windsor Castle*. The Great Western once again saw the publicity value of such a visit by allowing the King to drive the locomotive back from the works to Swindon station. Thereafter *Windsor Castle* became known on the Great Western as the 'Royal engine', being rostered for Royal duties on many future occasions.

The 'Castles' were generally completed in batches of 10. The first batch when new was fitted with 3,500gal tenders, the second batch was provided with intermediate type tenders of slightly higher capacity, but from engine No 5000 *Launceston Castle*, a new pattern of high sided tender was introduced. The new tenders had a coal capacity of 6 tons and a water capacity of 4,000gal, and fully loaded weighed 46ton 14cwt. The introduction of the new tenders gave the whole locomotive a better balanced look, and without doubt enhanced their appearance.

In 1926 No 5000 *Launceston Castle* was loaned to the London Midland & Scottish Railway where it ran trials between London and Carlisle. So successful were the trials, it is said that the LMS approached the Great Western with a view to Swindon constructing a batch of 'Castles' for use on the West Coast main line. History has it that the Great Western declined the offer. The 1932 batch of Nos 5023-5032, were constructed using a new technique of lining up the frames, cylinders and axle boxes using German made Ziess optical equipment. The earlier method was to use twine or fine wire to indicate the centre line. The higher standards of accuracy obtained by this new method resulted in a higher quality of construction, which in turn provided more economical running costs by increasing the mileage between repairs. Gradually usage of the class spread to cover many of the class one services on the system,

*Top:*
**This picture of No 4073 *Caerphilly Castle* approaching Knowle & Dorridge station circa 1925 is interesting as it shows quite clearly the spectacle-type cab windows that were fitted to the first 10 members of the class.** *M. Mensing collection*

*Above:*
**'Star' class No 4009 *Shooting Star* was constructed at Swindon in 1907. During 1925 it was rebuilt into a 'Castle', retaining the name and number, and is shown here shortly after conversion, complete with 3,500gal tender.** *Real Photos*

war austerity on the Great Western. An interesting feature on *Caerphilly* was the fitting of a sloping gutter to the cab roof. It was however, soon removed from the locomotive and was not fitted to further members of the class. The new engine was immediately placed on a variety of 'Star' rosters to prove to the civil engineers that it could perform satisfactorily on these turns, and once this had been established a further batch of nine 'Castles' was constructed at Swindon. These first 10 engines were all initially fitted with bogie brakes, but this

feature was soon removed, as were the high level spectacle type cab windows. This latter feature was removed on a gradual basis as and when the locomotives underwent boiler changes. One 'Star' detail retained on the first 20 'Castles' was the 'joggled' or set inward front main frames, to allow clearance for the front bogie wheels. From No 4093 and on all subsequent examples, straight frames were used, being 'dished' at the front to clear these wheels.

In September 1924 the Great Western's only Pacific, *The Great Bear* was rebuilt as a 'Castle'. Surprisingly it retained its old number, 111, but not its name, being renamed after the chairman of the company at the time, Viscount Churchill. The first 40 'Castles' were allocated between the Old Oak Common, Newton Abbot and Laira depots, from where they were put to work on the West of England services. It was on these services that the class gained its reputation for power, speed and economy. Dynamometer car tests undertaken by Collett during 1924 between Swindon and Plymouth using from Paddington to Penzance, Bristol, Chester and South Wales, but surprisingly they were not used on a regular basis over the new cut-off route between Paddington and Birmingham until about 1930.

During the 1930s the crack train on the Great Western was the 'Cheltenham Flyer', on which 'Castles' were performing superb high speed running on a daily basis. 'Castle' performances on this service reached their peak on 6 June 1932, when No 5006 *Tregenna Castle* covered the 77.3 miles from Swindon to Paddington in just 56min 47sec at an average speed of 81.68mph start to stop. It is interesting to include at this point an anecdote from Holcroft's work *An Outline of Great Western Locomotive Practice* where he relates a discussion between himself and a Running foreman at Swindon on the fine performances of the 'Castle' class on the up 'Cheltenham Flyer'. The train, remember, had a booked schedule of just 65 minutes for the 77.25 miles and was often run in less time. "Actually" replied the foreman "It is one of our easiest jobs. Holcroft then asked why the down run could not be attained in 65 minutes to which the reply came "Ah, that would be a very different matter". (There was in fact no corresponding down 'Cheltenham Flyer' service. The stock of the train, including the engine, travelled down as a semi-fast service.) Holcroft then suggested using a 'King' for the job, to which the foreman replied "As a matter of fact the 'Castle' is our best engine"!. Proof indeed that as long as the job was within its capacity, the running department acknowledged the 'Castles' as the number one express passenger class on the Great Western and not the 'Kings' as everyone supposed.

Speed was obviously of the essence at this time, for in 1935 a decision was made to fit all 'Castles' with speedometers. During the same year the Great Western succumbed to the streamlining craze by fitting No 5005 *Manorbier Castle* and No 6014 *King Henry VII*, with partial streamlining which included a horrendous bulbous nose. The bits and pieces that were added completely ruined the fine lines and balanced looks of both locomotives, but apparently had little effect on improving wind resistance. Thankfully the experiment was abandoned, and over the next few years the streamlining was gradually removed, although No 5005 retained its special type of shifting valve right up until withdrawal. Collett's explanation of the termination of the experiment mentions that the streamlining caused overheating of the bearings and had a detrimental effect on both coal and oil consumption. He does not mention the detrimental effect to the looks of the two locomotives, but I suspect this also had something to do with the decision. Whilst on the subject

*Left*:
On 17 February 1936 No 4009 was renamed *Lloyds* and numbered 100 A1. It is seen here during the following year at Bathford halt on what is probably an ex-works running-in turn. *Real Photos*

*Below*:
No 111 *Viscount Churchill*, the *Great Bear* rebuild, heads the 12 noon express from Penzance to Manchester (London Road) past Ponsandane box on 15 June 1951. *P. J. Kelley*

of speed the first 'Castle' officially to record a speed of 100mph was No 4086 *Builth Castle*, descending Honeybourne Bank with the 12.45pm Paddington-Worcester service on 31 July 1939.

From about 1936 a shorter pattern chimney was introduced and although it was extensively fitted to many of the class some retained the original high pattern chimney until well after Nationalisation.

The class was proving to be so successful that between 1937 and 1940 Collett had no less than 10 of the 12 'Star' class 'Abbeys' rebuilt as 'Castles'. This required amongst other things a lengthening of the frames, and this was achieved by simply welding on new pieces of frame at the cab end, fitting a new No 8 boiler in place of the No 1, and fitting a new enlarged cab. Interestingly these 10 rebuilds were considered and charged by the company as completely new locomotives. The 'Abbey' rebuilds were not as successful as one would imagine, for they always gave trouble throughout their working lives, principally from cracked frames. Apart from this inherent problem, many drivers also considered that overall they were not up to the standard of the rest of the class.

Collett retired in July 1941, by which date there were some 131 'Castle' class in service. In October 1946 No 5091 *Cleeve Abbey* was converted to burn oil. Four other 'Castles' were similarly treated: Nos 5039 and 5083 in December 1946 and Nos 100A1 and 5079 in January 1947. As oil burners the engine weight was increased by about one ton, mainly due to the extra brick lining in the firebox. The tender laden weight also rose by about six tons when carrying 1,950gal of fuel oil and 4,000gal of water. The scheme however was short-lived and the five were converted back to burn coal during the autumn of 1948. The potential use of oil as substitute fuel was still being actively considered by the Western Region during the mid-1950s with a proposal to convert a considerable number of ex-Great Western locomotives, including a large number of 'Castles', into oil burners. A completely new type of oil burning apparatus had been developed at Swindon for this purpose, but the decision to build the new 'Warship' class diesel-hydraulics saw the project finally abandoned in January 1959.

Such was the success of the 'Castles' that Collett's successor F. W. Hawksworth had no hesitation in resuming construction once World War 2 had ended. Hawksworth's improvements included fitting high temperature Schmidt three-row superheaters in place of the old Swindon low temperature types, and the provision of mechanical lubrication for the cylinders, valves and throttle. Also from No 7008 a new type of straight-sided

tender, weighing 49 tons loaded, was introduced. Another alteration undertaken by Hawksworth was the fitting in September 1947, of a new type of boiler to No 5049 *Earl of Plymouth*. The new boiler contained a four-row superheater which produced a super-heat temperature of some 660°F. In order to accommodate the rather bulky superheater header the chimney was moved forward by about eight inches. The subsequent reduction in water consumption coupled to a longer

boiler life saw this type of boiler gradually introduced to other members of the class from about 1953. To compensate for the decline in the quality of coal being supplied during the period after World War 2, 'Castle' smokeboxes were modified to provide improved draughting. The alterations required a reduction in the chimney liner and blast-pipe diameters, together with the removal of the Churchward 'jumper top' on the blastpipe. Those 'Castles' so modified were externally unchanged but had a small 'Improved Draughting' plate fitted in the cab.

'Castle' class construction came to an end in August 1950 with the construction of No 7037, some 27 years to the month after the completion of the prototype. No 7037 was officially named *Swindon* on 15 November 1950 by HRH the Princess Elizabeth during an official visit to commemorate the golden jubilee of the borough. The class eventually comprised 171 locomotives of which 155 were constructed from new. Apart from a break in production during the war years, 'Castles' had been in almost continuous production from August 1923 to August 1950, a record for any express passenger type and a tribute to Collett's original design.

Once production had ceased thoughts at Swindon turned to improving the breed. During 1954 a new more curved design of outside steam pipe was introduced, replacing the original pattern which was prone to the occasional fracture. In December 1955 6017 *King Edward IV* was successfully fitted

*Above:*
**This interesting line-up was taken at Swindon, probably for publicity purposes, on 7 December 1933. It shows four 'Castles' and three 'Kings' supposedly being prepared for the day's work. The 'Castle' in the foreground carries the 'Cheltenham Flyer' headboard.** *Great Western Trust*

with a double (twin orifice) blast pipe and chimney, and following this success, in May 1956, No 7018 *Drysllwyn Castle,* which at the time had a three row superheater boiler, was also fitted with a double blast pipe and an experimental double chimney, the latter being fabricated from sheet steel. Subsequent tests showed a great improvement to what had previously been a rather indifferent performer. The final modification to the class came with the fitting in March 1957 to No 4090 *Dorchester Castle* of a four-row superheater boiler, double blast-pipe and new design double chimney, the latter being constructed from cast iron. Such was the improvement in both steaming and performance ('Castles' so fitted could produce some 3,600lb of pull at 86mph on 20% cut off) that a total of 66 'Castles' were so modified. There is no doubt that these modifications gave an extended life to many examples of the class. In 1958 No 7018 *Drysllwyn Castle* was itself fitted with a four-row superheater, and the new type blast

pipe and double chimney. These modifications, together with a greatly improved mechanical lubrication system, finally turned a locomotive which had once been the proverbial ugly duckling into quite a swan, for on 28 April 1958, whilst working on the up 'Bristolian', *Drysllwyn* with seven coaches, ran the 117.6 miles to

Paddington in the record time of 93min 50sec, easily topping the 100mph mark at Somerford. Just to prove the point, it again equalled its record time on 2 May with an eight coach train. On each occasion No 7018 was driven by Jimmy Russe from the Bath Road Shed. The 'Castles', it seemed, had reached their finest hour.

*Right:*
**The 'Cheltenham Flyer' at speed near Cholsey on 19 May 1936.**
*Great Western Trust*

*Left:*
Sporting its newly acquired double chimney, No 7018 *Drysllwyn Castle* stands at Paignton in July 1956 with the up 'Torbay Express'. The locomotive is under test. Following the fitting of the double blastpipe and chimney, hence the dynamometer car next to the tender. *Ian Allan Library*

*Centre left:*
The 10.40am Sundays only service from Liverpool to Plymouth, hauled by No 5078 *Beaufort*, is seen approaching Uphill Junction, south of Weston-super-Mare in the early 1950s. *W. N. Lockett*

*Bottom left:*
A diverted Pembroke Dock-Paddington service makes a spectacular sight as it climbs the final 1 in 60 stretch up to Sapperton tunnel, double-headed by Nos 7035 *Ogmore Castle* and 5051 *Earl Bathurst* in December 1951. *G. F. Heiron*

*Above right:*
Little and large meet at Ealing Broadway as No 7002 *Devizes Castle* on a Paddington-Fishguard service roars past No 1426 on the Ealing-Greenford branch auto-train on 5 February 1952. *P. J. Kelley*

*Right:*
Two very youthful spotters watch No 5045 *Earl of Dudley* as it arrives at Leamington Spa on 25 August 1952 with a through service from Wolverhampton to Weymouth. *B. Morrison*

*Below:*
A lovely shot of No 5055 *Earl of Eldon* leaving Box tunnel with the 9.15am service from Paddington to Bristol on 8 September 1952. The tiny halt at Box (Mill Lane) can just be seen behind the rear coach of the train. *G. F. Heiron*

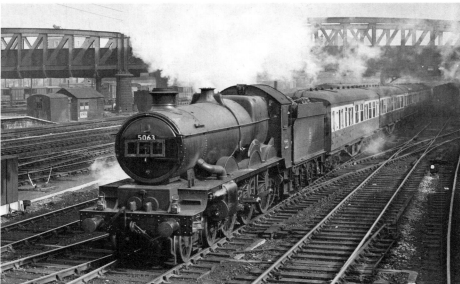

*Left:*
The North & West route provided a fine stamping ground for the 'Castles' over the years. Here a Liverpool-Plymouth express hauled by No 5073 *Blenheim* passes Penpergwm (Abergavenny) on 27 September 1952. *J. F. Russell-Smith*

*Below left:*
No 5063 *Earl Baldwin*, complete with red-backed name and numberplates, leaves Paddington with a service to Worcester on 10 October 1950. *Ian Allan Library*

*Bottom:*
The 9.20am service from Bournemouth West to Birkenhead is seen leaving Shrewsbury on 1 June 1953 hauled by No 5070 *Sir Daniel Gooch*. The locomotive is fitted with a black tender. *L. N. Owen*

*Top right:*
The last express passenger locomotive to be built by the GWR was 'Castle' No 7007 *Ogmore Castle*. To commemorate the event it was renamed *Great Western* in January 1948. It is seen on 17 July 1953 leaving Oxford with the 11.00am service from Hereford to Paddington. *E. D. Bruton*

*Centre right:*
The 1.30pm service from Sheffield Victoria to Cardiff hauled by No 5009 *Shrewsbury Castle* is seen passing Kennington Junction, south of Oxford on Saturday 18 July 1953. The 'Castle' would have replaced an Eastern Region locomotive at Banbury, and apart from the BR Mk 1 coach, the remaining stock appears to be of LNER origin. *E. D. Bruton*

*Bottom right:*
No 7016 *Chester Castle*, complete with a set of Southern stock, heads through the chalk hills of Wiltshire with a Bristol-Salisbury stopping train in April 1954. *Author's collection*

**Left:**
Framed nicely in the arch of the Shaldon Bridge No 5058 *Earl of Clancarty* skirts the estuary wall at Teignmouth with the down 'Cornishman' on 16 July 1955.  *L. Elsey*

**Inset:**
The up 'South Wales Pullman' enters the original station at Port Talbot General behind No 4095 *Harlech Castle* on 15 May 1956.  *Great Western Trust*

**Top right:**
No 7000 *Viscount Portal* makes a superb sight as it leaves picturesque Kingswear on the evening of 8 July 1956, with the 6.20pm service to Exeter St Davids.  *P. J. Kelley*

**Centre right:**
Echoes of summers past are recalled as No 5046 *Earl Cawdor* heads the 11.20am service from Newton Abbot to Kingswear, between Goodrington and Churston on 8 July 1956. The eventual restoration of No 7027 *Thornbury Castle*, currently at Buckfastleigh, may once again see this scene repeated.  *P. J. Kelley*

**Below:**
No 5078 *Beaufort* leans into the curve as it nears Kingskerswell with the 9.10am service from Manchester (London Road) to Paignton on 11 August 1956.  *P. F. Bowles*

*Left:*
The 9.10am Liverpool-Plymouth through service accelerates away from Shrewsbury on 2 March 1957 behind No 5079 *Lysander*. *Ian Allan Library*

*Below left:*
No 7023 *Penrice Castle* approaches All Stretton halt on the climb to Church Stretton with the 3.00pm service from Liverpool to Cardiff on Whit Monday 10 June 1957. *M. Mensing*

*Centre left:*
No 5013 *Abergavenny Castle*, diverted due to engineering work, passes Copper Pit platform on the Morriston branch with a Sunday Paddington-Swansea service, circa 1957. *J. D. Edwards*

*Bottom left:*
No 4098 *Kidwelly Castle* speeds through Kingskerswell with the down 'Torbay Express' on 29 June 1957. *P. F. Bowles*

*Right:*
No 5053 *Earl Cairns* makes a superb sight as it crosses Greenway Viaduct, between Kingswear and Churston, with a return excursion to Bristol on 8 September 1957. *D. S. Fish*

*Below:*
No 4085 *Berkeley Castle* arrives at Evesham on Sunday 9 March 1958 with the 12.20pm Oxford-Worcester stopping service. The two-coach train appears to be rather over-powered. *M. Mensing*

*Left:*
No 4095 *Harlech Castle* awaits departure from Penzance, with the up 'Royal Duchy', the 11.00am service to Paddington, on Easter Monday 1958.  *P. Q. Treloar*

*Centre left:*
An amateur photographers' excursion from Paddington to Stratford-upon-Avon, hauled by No 5007 *Rougemont Castle*, passes Pebworth halt on the Honeybourne-Stratford line on Sunday 18 May 1958. *M. Mensing*

*Bottom left:*
No 5026 *Criccieth Castle* passes the small goods yard at Beaconsfield with the 07.20 Pwllheli-Paddington service on 2 August 1958.  *J. D. Edwards*

*Right:*
Dusk at Paddington as No 5005 *Manorbier Castle* awaits departure with a service to Swindon and Gloucester, circa 1959. *D. Sellman*

*Below:*
No 5023 *Brecon Castle* passes West London sidings on the down 'Royal Duchy', whilst No 5095 *Barbury Castle* runs up to Paddington via the overbridge line to power the 1.50pm service to Carmarthen. *R. C. Riley*

*Bottom right:*
No 5084 *Reading Abbey* speeds through Widney Manor station with the up 'Cambrian Coast Express' on 18 April 1959. The locomotive is fitted with a double chimney and an oil consumption gauge. *M. Mensing*

**Left:**
No 5021 *Whittington Castle* climbs to Gwinear Road with the 11.50am 'Royal Duchy' service from Penzance to Paddington on Saturday 4 July 1959. *P. Q. Treloar*

**Centre left:**
The early autumn sunshine highlights No 5050 *Earl of St Germans* as it pulls away from Dawlish with the 9.15am service from Liverpool and Manchester to Plymouth in September 1959. *A. A. Sellman*

**Bottom:**
The up 'Devonian' hauled by No 5055 *Earl of Eldon* passes new 'Warship' diesel-hydraulic No D806 *Cambrian* at Newton Abbot in September 1959. *D. S. Fish*

**Right:**
The 8.00am through service from Paignton to Manchester Victoria pulls away from Exeter St Davids behind No 5032 *Usk Castle* in September 1959. *A. A. Sellman*

**Centre right:**
No 5066 *Sir Felix Pole* emerges from Kennaway tunnel, Dawlish, with the 9.15am Kingswear-Paddington in September 1959. *A. A. Sellman*

**Bottom right:**
Easy work for a double chimney 'Castle' as No 7004 *Eastnor Castle* heads an up milk service between Stoneycombe and Aller Junction in September 1959. *D. Cross*

*Above:*
The 'William Shakespeare', the 10.10am service from Paddington to Wolverhampton, here hauled by No 5060 *Earl of Berkeley* approaches Gerrards Cross on 6 June 1951. This service was inaugurated especially for the 1951 Festival of Britain and carried through coaches for Stratford-upon-Avon, hence the name. *Author's Collection*

*Left:*
Dennis Compton (the 'Brylcreem man') appears to be looking approvingly at No 5058 *Earl of Clancarty* as it simmers quietly at Penzance after working in with the 'Cornish Riviera' express on 10 September 1952. *L. Overend*

*Below left:*
During the Coronation year (1953) Western Region named-expresses carried special ER II headboards, as can be seen in this picture of No 7017 *G. J. Churchward* as it waits to take over the up 'Red Dragon' at Cardiff General from fellow 'Castle' No 7020 *Gloucester Castle* on 4 June 1953. *E. Mountford*

*Above right:*
The up 'Torbay Express' hauled by No 5079 *Lysander* leaves Churston in the summer of 1953, whilst in the bay 0-4-2T No 1466, now at Didcot Railway Centre, prepares to leave with the push-pull service to Brixham. *R. Hewitt*

*Right:*
The down 'South Wales Pullman' hauled by No 5006 *Tregenna Castle* heads past Newport Ebbw Junction on 26 August 1960. *G. England*

*Above:*
Passengers stand patiently under Francis Fox's superb roof, as the stock of the 4.30pm non-stop service to Paddington, the 'Bristolian', arrives at Bristol Temple Meads behind No 5085 *Evesham Abbey*. Fellow 'Castle' No 7037 *Swindon* awaits the arrival of the 1.12pm service from Plymouth to Liverpool, which it will take northwards.
*J. D. Edwards*

*Far left:*
No 5059 *Earl St Aldwyn* passes Abbey Foregate Junction signalbox as it departs from Shrewsbury on Saturday 24 September 1960 with the up 'Cambrian Coast Express'.  *Dr G. Smith*

*Left:*
No 7006 *Lydford Castle* runs into Exeter St Davids with the 'Royal Duchy', the 1.30pm service from Paddington to Penzance, in September 1959.  *D. Sellman*

*Above:*
**The down 'Cheltenham Spa Express' hauled by No 7035 *Ogmore Castle* passes the large motive power depot at Southall 1960. With the constant renaming of the 'Castles' over the years, the name *Ogmore Castle* ended up being carried on no less than four different locomotives.** *J. D. Edwards*

*Right:*
**No 7011 *Banbury Castle* complete with a beautifully clean rake of chocolate & cream Mk 1 coaches leaves the Cotswold Line at Wolvercote Junction, north of Oxford, with the up 'Cathedrals Express', the 9.50am service from Hereford in June 1961.**
*Dr G. Smith*

*Above:*
The lovely garden at Bruton station makes a fine setting for No 7017 *G. J. Churchward* as it passes with the 8.15am Paddington-Minehead on 18 August 1962.
*Peter Fry/Great Western Trust*

*Right:*
No 5092 *Tresco Abbey* sweeps through Hullavington on 25 November 1961 with the 7.30am service Swansea-Paddington.
*Peter Fry/Great Western Trust*.

# Castles
## AT SPEED

**Right:**
The fine lines of the single chimney 'Castles' are shown to good effect as No 5012 *Berry Pomeroy Castle* of Oxford shed, rushes past Bentley Heath on 27 December 1960 with a through service from Birkenhead to Bournemouth.
*M. Mensing*

**Below:**
A hard working No 5075 *Wellington* speeds the 11.45am Sunday service from Birkenhead to Paddington past Widney Manor on 23 June 1957. *M. Mensing*

**Below right:**
No 5044 *Earl of Dunraven* at speed near Widney Manor with the 6.00pm service from Paddington to Gobowen on Sunday 19 May 1957. *M. Mensing*

**Bottom right:**
No 5029 *Nunney Castle* approaches Solihull with the 7.25am service from Wolverhampton to Paddington on 31 July 1959. *M. Mensing*

*Left:*
No 7034 *Ince Castle* passes Stonehouse, Gloucs, on 13 October 1962 with the 8.00am service from Cheltenham St James to Paddington, the 'Cheltenham Spa Express'. *Peter Fry/Great Western Trust*

*Below left:*
No 5091 *Cleeve Abbey*, recently out of the paint shop, stands outside Swindon Works on 20 May 1962. *A. Doyle*

*Right:*
No 7029 *Clun Castle* (now preserved) runs through Sonning cutting with down milk empties on 31 August 1961. *A. Doyle*

*Below:*
The left-hand nameplate of No 7005, pictured at Oxford in 1962. One of the nameplates from No 7005 is currently on display at the Elgar Birthplace Museum near Worcester. *D. Tuck*

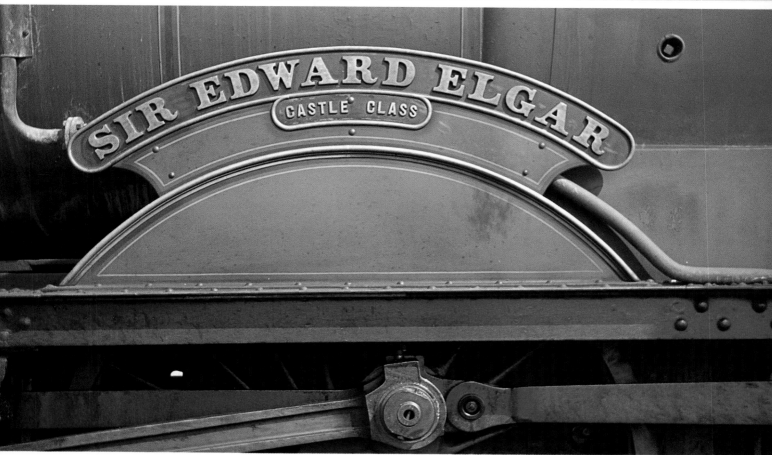

# Chapter Two

## THE FINAL YEARS

The construction at Swindon during 1958 of the first 'Warship' class diesel-hydraulics probably sent ominous shivers down the spine of many 'Castle' enthusiasts since these locomotives were constructed as 'Castle' replacements. From 27 July 1959 the 'Bristolian' and the 'Torbay Express', both regular 'Castle' workings, succumbed to diesel power. However with the poor reliability record of the diesel-hydraulics, particularly in the first few years, the 'Castles' continued to prove their worth, providing the main motive power on services to South Wales, Worcester and the West to North route.

It is worth mentioning at this point the 5.35pm Oxford-Paddington service, for this was probably the fastest scheduled 'Castle' working during the early 1960s. Worked by Oxford men the train was usually powered by either an Oxford or Wolverhampton-based member of the class. The 60min allowance for the 63.5 mile run from Oxford included a booked time of just 49.5min for the 52.66 miles from Didcot East Junction to Paddington. Oxford men obviously enjoyed working this turn, with many of the drivers relating that this was the one chance in their roster of really having a go. Some excellent times were put up over the years, one such example in April 1962 (shortly before the service was dieselised), saw 5001 Llandovery Castle (with double chimney) complete the distance in just 53min 9sec, at an average speed of 71.7mph.

It was during this same year that another remarkable 'Castle' run was made. Prior to the acceleration of services over the 'cut-off route' between Paddington and Birmingham, and in order to ascertain the condition of the track, the Western Region ran a high speed test train on 15 May 1962 using No 7030 Cranbrook Castle and five coaches. On the down journey Cranbrook Castle, which prior to the run had spent some weeks in store at Old Oak Common, touched 96mph at Haddenham, but it was on the up journey that Cranbrook really surpassed itself speed-wise, hitting 103mph at both Blackthorn and Denham, the highest speed ever recorded for the class.

During the early 1960s 'Castles' were still the mainstay of motive power on

such services as the 'South Wales Pullman', the 'Cheltenham Spa Express', the 'Pembroke Coast Express', the 'Red Dragon' and the 'Cathedrals Express'. This latter service was the last named train on the Western Region to be fully dieselised, remaining predominantly 'Castle'-hauled until the autumn of 1963

Gradually, however, as further 'Warships', 3,500hp 'Hymeks' and 2,700hp 'Westerns', were introduced, the 'Castles' were relegated to secondary duties. Up to the end of 1961 only 10 examples of the class had been withdrawn, but increasing diesel deliveries saw 55 'Castles' removed from service during 1962, and by the end of the year the only regular daily Class 1 passenger turns for 'Castle' class locomotives were on the Paddington-Worcester services. In January 1963 Worcester shed

had nine examples Nos 7001/3/4/7/13/23/25/27/31, to cover these duties. Gradually as the months passed, the 'Hymek' diesel-hydraulics took over the services and from Sunday 8 September 1963 steam was withdrawn from the Paddington-Worcester trains. The last official Class 1 'Castle' turn from Worcester took place on Saturday 7 September when No 7023 Penrice Castle headed the 11.10am up service

*Below:*
**The small yard at Ranelagh Bridge, just outside Paddington was used for servicing locomotives requiring a quick turn-round between duties. On 29 January 1957 No 7026 Tenby Castle is seen alongside the turntable, whilst in the background another 'Castle', a 'King' and 'Britannia' No 70016 Ariel await their next turn of duty.** *P. J. Kelley*

to Paddington, and apart from the occasional fill-in for a diesel failure, that should have been that as far as 'Castles' were concerned on the Worcester expresses. However, during the spring of 1964 'Castles' returned to these services once again, albeit for just a few weeks, and during their stay some lucky travellers were even treated to 100mph running down Honeybourne Bank. The reason for this remarkable turn of events was the decision by the Western Region in March 1964 to commemorate the 60th anniversary of the *City of Truro* high speed run with a 'Castle'-hauled, Paddington-Plymouth-Paddington railtour which would be run at high speed. The whole event was jointly organised by the Western Region and publishers Ian Allan. The subsequent testing for this event, in order to find suitable locomotives, saw 'Castles' reintroduced on to the Worcester services.

The idea of using 'Castles' for the high speed run was all very well on paper but in practice it must be remembered that by March 1964 there were only 28 members of the class still operational. Also the servicing of any steam

locomotive on the Western at this time was being undertaken on a patch-up basis, and to provide any 'Castle' that was in good enough order to run up to 100mph was asking rather a lot. The engine record sheets disclose that it had been almost two years since any of them had visited Swindon Works for an overhaul. Such was the quality of the 'Castles', even in a rundown form, that eight of the remaining survivors were considered potentially good enough to hit the magic 100. In the weeks preceding the run, locomotive inspectors had travelled on all the remaining 'Castles' that had run under 40,000 miles since their last overhaul, in order to assess their capabilities and to produce a shortlist of the best eight. Once these were selected they were sent to either Worcester or Swindon motive power depots to have their valves, piston and valve gear removed and examined, and at the same time have any other defects rectified. One of those selected, No 5057 *Earl Waldegrave*, was soon removed from the list when it was found to have cracked cylinder liners. After some deliberation it was eventually replaced by No 4079 *Pendennis Castle* which had originally been omitted because of its age, but subsequent testing found it to be in excellent condition. After each locomotive was examined it was placed on the 9.15am Paddington-Worcester service and the

1.15pm return. In his article in the *Great Western Echo*, the late Jack Hancock who at the time was the Chief Locomotive Inspector on the Western Region, states that the Paddington-Worcester service was chosen as a testbed for three reasons. Firstly because steam locomotives were still being used on the route, secondly because Didcot, Worcester and presumably Oxford men were still conversant with steam and thirdly because the inspectors who had to make the final choice could set up all the test conditions on this route. The testing itself was to ascertain (i) the general condition of the locomotive (ii) if the locomotive being tested could maintain steam pressure and boiler level using the exhaust injector whilst being worked constantly in the 25% cut off, and with full regulator opening and (iii) if it was capable of sustained high speed running. The locomotives finally selected for these tests were Nos 4079, 5054, 7008, 7022, 7023, 7025, 7029 and 7032. The task was to find the three best examples with three reserves, and testing commenced on 21 March with No 7032. This was followed by No 7029 on 24 March, 5054 on 1 April, 7025 on 2nd, 4079 on 4th, 7008 on 20th, 7023 on 21st and finally 7022 on 27 April. It was general practice on the Western Region in operating the 'Castles' at high speed to use a cut-off of between 15-17%, so it was no surprise to the

*Left:*
No 4082 *Windsor Castle* makes a fine sight as it leaves Oxford with the 11.10am service from Worcester to Paddington in May 1962. *A. Doyle*

*Below left:*
No 5054 *Earl of Ducie* on the OURS 'Castle Farewell' special at Patchway on 16 May 1964. *Peter Fry/Great Western Trust*

*Right:*
No 7022 *Hereford Castle* passes Wolvercote Siding on 25 July 1964 with a train load of concrete sleepers. *A. Doyle*

*Below:*
No 7023 *Penrice Castle* leaves Bath Green Park with a return RCTS special to Gloucester on 7 June 1964. *Peter Fry/Great Western Trust*

*Left:*
No 5095 *Barbury Castle* is seen here being prepared at Shrewsbury shed in readiness for duty on the 'Cambrian Coast Express' on 28 July 1961. *A. R. Forrest*

*Below left:*
The rather scruffy atmosphere of a typical shed yard is well portrayed in this photo of Worcester, where on Sunday 19 August 1962 No 5099 *Clifford Castle* is seen being prepared to work the 5.40pm service to London. *M. Mensing*

must be said that the 'Castles' performed superbly and proved once and for all what magnificent machines they were. The following extract about the run from Plymouth to Bristol is reproduced from the *Great Western Echo* by kind permission of the Great Western Society. The three man crew comprised Firemen Watts and Rundell and Driver Harry Roach who described the run.

*'On leaving Plymouth, my first job was to get a couple of minutes in hand by Hemerdon because of the speed restriction at Monksmoor Bridge, Wrangaton. The locomotive No 7029, was in good condition and no trouble was experienced in steaming. By Newton I had a couple of minutes in hand but adverse signals at Hackney nearly brought me to a stand. Afterwards I found out the 4pm from Plymouth was just in front of me. I also had the 'Distant' against me at both Teignmouth and Starcross but I had done well as I was still right on time when passing through Exeter. I noticed the 4pm in the platform and with the backboards off I let the locomotive have her head. The way she climbed up the Exe valley was a treat. I even had to ease her on the rising 1 in 200 between Hele & Bradninch and Cullompton for the 65mph restriction at milepost 183. The rest of the climb was very good and I entered Whiteball Tunnel a good 8mph faster than the City of Truro. Bearing the instructions of the general manager in mind, it was a case of holding the train back. I have no doubt whatsoever that had I have been permitted I would have beaten the* City of Truro's *record. After passing Taunton I had to ease for the 40mph restriction at Cogload when crossing from the Up 'Berks Hants' to the Bristol road and in the short distance to Durston I was doing nearly 60mph, at Bridgwater 80 and all the way to Bristol the needle was above the 90 mark'.*

One of the firemen commented after the run 'The engine was very free and no effort was required to keep her steaming. The hardest job in fact was holding her back'. Remember that during the tests Inspector Hancock had only rated No 7029 as the third best 'Castle'!

The final part of the run, from Bristol to Paddington, used No 5054 *Earl of Ducie*, fitted with a single chimney.

mechanical engineers that the use of a 25% cut-off and a full regulator caused injector problems, as six of the eight were unable to maintain adequate boiler water level using the exhaust injector alone, so on these the right-hand injector was also used. This necessitated the exhaust injectors being removed from these six engines and sent to Swindon for repair. As each locomotive was refitted it was re-tested and eventually after a total 14 evaluation trips the final order of preference made by the inspectors was Nos 5054, 4079, 7029, 7023, 7008, 7032, 7022 and 7025.

Rostering for the 9 May Special saw No 4079 on the Paddington-Plymouth leg, No 7029 on the Plymouth-Bristol section and No 5054 on the final leg from Bristol to Paddington. On each leg the crew would comprise a driver and two firemen. London men were selected to work to Plymouth, Plymouth men from Plymouth to Bristol and Bristol men to London.

The first leg of the run was marred when No 4079 *Pendennis Castle* dropped its firebars near Lavington at 96mph. Afterwards it was found that the firebars were porous and that the extra heat obtained from the Ogilvie coal that was being used on the day, had caused them to melt. Unfortunately the magic 100mph figure was not achieved during the day, but overall it

## W.R. "GREAT WESTERN" PLYMOUTH-BRISTOL

Engine: 4-cyl. 4-6-0 No. 7029 *Clun Castle.*
Load: 7 coaches, 243 tons tare, 265 tons gross.

| Dist. | | Sched. | Actual | Speeds |
|---|---|---|---|---|
| miles | | min. | m. s. | m.p.h. |
| 0.00 | PLYMOUTH | 0 | 0.00 | — |
| 1.50 | Lipson Junc. | 3½ | 3.45 | * |
| 4.05 | Plympton | — | 6.43 | 47½ |
| 6.70 | Hemerdon | 14½ | 11.22 | 23½ |
| 10.80 | Ivybridge | — | 16.42 | 52 |
| | | | p.w.s. | *15 |
| 14.10 | Wrangaton | — | 21.59 | † |
| 16.30 | Brent | 26 | 24.38 | *53 |
| 18.60 | Rattery | — | 27.10 | 58† |
| 23.15 | Totnes | 34 | 32.20 | *46† |
| 27.95 | Dainton | — | 39.10 | 30½/† |
| 30.75 | Aller Junc. | 46 | 42.50 | *50 |
| 31.85 | NEWTON ABBOT | 48 | 44.20 | *30 |
| | | | sigs. | *15/*20 |
| 37.00 | Teignmouth | — | 52.05 | *20 |
| 39.85 | Dawlish | — | 57.08 | *40 |
| 41.50 | Dawlish Warren | 60 | 59.07 | *40 |
| 43.55 | Starcross | — | 61.32 | *47 |
| 47.25 | Exminster | — | 65.37 | 64 |
| 51.15 | St. Thomas | — | 69.25 | — |
| 52.05 | EXETER | 71 | 70.52 | *30 |
| 53.30 | Cowley Bridge Junc. | 73 | 72.42 | 48 |
| 55.45 | Stoke Canon | — | 74.57 | 61 |
| 60.45 | Hele | — | 79.22 | 76½/*62 |
| 64.65 | Cullompton | — | 82.57 | 69/65 |
| 66.85 | Tiverton Junc. | — | 84.59 | 70½ |
| 68.65 | Sampford Peverell | — | 86.27 | 77½ |
| 71.95 | Whiteball | 93 | 89.12 | 70½/92 |
| 75.70 | Wellington | — | 91.52 | *82/96 |
| 80.85 | Vorton Fitzwarren | — | 95.27 | — |
| 82.80 | TAUNTON | 100½ | 96.49 | *82 |
| 85.25 | Creech Junc. | — | 98.15 | 83½ |
| 87.55 | Cogload | — | 100.31 | *45 |
| 88.60 | Durston | — | 101.47 | 58 |
| 94.35 | BRIDGEWATER | 112 | 106.35 | 83½ |
| 96.90 | Dunball | — | 108.26 | 82 |
| 100.65 | Highbridge | 117½ | 111.05 | 87½ |
| 103.40 | Brent Knoll | — | 113.02 | 88 |
| 107.90 | Uphill Junc. | 123½ | 116.09 | 90 |
| 110.80 | Worle Junc. | 126 | 117.59 | 90 |
| 115.60 | YATTON | — | 121.12 | 90 |
| 119.55 | Nailsea | — | 123.50 | 92 |
| 121.70 | Flax Bourton | — | 125.25 | 75 |
| 125.55 | Parson Street | — | 128.47 | * |
| 126.50 | Bedminster | — | 130.00 | * |
| 127.40 | BRISTOL T.M. | 143 | 133.09 | — |

* Speed restriction. † Continuous speed restrictions, Ivybridge to Starcross. Net time, Plymouth-Bristol, 128min.

Inspector Jack Hancock who had been responsible for the testing of the locomotives just a few weeks earlier was on the footplate. His description of the run, is again taken from the *Great Western Echo* and makes interesting reading.

"The timing shown in the July 1964 edition of the *Railway World* from Bristol start to Paddington stop is 95min 33sec, whilst my log shows 95min 18sec and it is probable that the difference was brought about by the fact that, as we received the 'right away' signal and Driver Higby gave a long blast on the whistle, there was a terrific explosion of steam, and as this coincided with the opening of the regulator, everyone on the footplate wore shocked expressions wondering what had happened, and we momentarily froze into immobility, and I forgot to press the button of my stop watch. It was in fact the bursting of the steam heating pipe between the tender and the first coach. I gave instructions for the steam heating valve to be closed and decided that the enthusiasm of the passengers in the train would have to be sufficient to keep them warm. Anyway, as there no doubt was a considerable number of windows open in any case, it would be almost a waste of steam which could be put to better use, and as we shall see later, this probably contributed to the failure to achieve the desired 100mph.

"There is a PROS (permanent restriction of speed) of 10mph out of Bristol Temple Meads, and another one of 15mph from there to Dr Day's Bridge Junction: and I think that we adhered to them fairly well, but as soon as we passed Dr Day's we really got cracking. By the time we passed Stapleton Road we were doing 40mph with the valve travel at the 40% cut-off. This as you know is pretty heavy and the sparks were really belting up the chimney. Through Ashley Hill the gradient steepens to 1 in 75 and the regulator was opened wider and the valve travel extended but in spite of this the speed dropped to 36mph. As we approached Filton and passed the summit we eased the regulator to a 25% opening in order to keep the speed within the maximum allowable, passing the signalbox 1 minute inside the booked schedule. We sailed round to Stoke Gifford and now joined the South Wales line to London. The gradient is rising continuously 1 in 300 to Badminton which is a distance of 11.75 miles, and was passed in 11 minutes, giving an average speed of 64mph. The regulator was now 75% open with the valve travel at 35% cut-off. I have never seen more enthusiastic firemen than Ray Gitson and Cliff Richards, and they were continually urging Driver Higby to go faster, although it meant them

*Above left:*
No 5070 *Sir Daniel Gooch* passes Fairwood Junction signalbox at Westbury with the 10.10am up relief service from Torquay on 8 June 1963.
*Peter Fry/Great Western Trust*

*Left:*
No 7011 *Banbury Castle* prepares to leave Paddington with the 'Cathedrals Express' in October 1962.   *A. Doyle*

*Above:*
No 7007 *Great Western* at Oxford with a down Worcester service on 22 June 1962.
*S. Boorne*

*Right:*
No 5097 *Sarum Castle* hurries through Freshford Halt with the 12.50pm service from Cardiff to Brighton on 22 April 1962.
*Peter Fry/Great Western Trust*

## W.R. "GREAT WESTERN" BRISTOL–PADDINGTON

Engine: 4-cyl. 4-6-0 No. 5054, *Earl of Ducie*.
Load: 7 coaches, 243 tons tare, 265 tons gross.

| Dist. | | Sched. | Actual | Speeds |
|---|---|---|---|---|
| miles | | min. | m. s. | m.p.h. |
| 0.00 | BRISTOL T.M. | 0 | 0.00 | — |
| 0.60 | Dr. Days | | | |
| | Bridge Junc. | — | 2.38 | *15 |
| 1.65 | Stapleton | | | |
| | Road | 5 | 4.24 | 45 |
| 2.50 | Ashley Hill | — | 5.39 | 42 |
| 3.90 | Horfield | — | 7.25 | 37 |
| 4.80 | FILTON | | | |
| | JUNC. | 9½ | 8.56 | 48 |
| 6.20 | Stoke Gifford | | | |
| | East | 11½ | 10.30 | 50 |
| 9.20 | Coalpit Heath | — | 13.39 | 63 |
| 13.10 | Chipping | | | |
| | Sodbury | — | 17.12 | 69/70 |
| 17.65 | BADMINTON | 22½ | 21.12 | 66 |
| 23.40 | Hullavington | — | 25.54 | 89 |
| 27.90 | Little | | | |
| | Somerford | — | 28.30 | 96 |
| 30.65 | Brinkworth | — | 30.17 | 88 |
| 34.75 | Wootton | | | |
| | Bassett | 35 | 33.28 | *65 |
| 40.35 | SWINDON | 39½ | 37.57 | 80 |
| 46.15 | Shrivenham | — | 42.04 | 86 |
| 51.15 | Uffington | 47½ | 45.31 | 90 |
| 53.85 | Challow | — | 47.18 | 88 |
| 57.25 | Wantage Road | — | 49.39 | 88 |
| 61.15 | Steventon | 54½ | 52.17 | 87 |
| 64.55 | DIDCOT | 57 | 54.36 | 87 |
| 69.20 | Cholsey | — | 57.55 | 84 |
| 72.90 | Goring | — | 60.37 | 80 |
| 76.10 | Pangbourne | — | 63.00 | *79 |
| 79.00 | Tilehurst | — | 65.08 | 82/84 |
| 81.65 | READING | 69 | 67.05 | *79/81 |
| 86.65 | Twyford | 73 | 70.49 | *75 |
| 93.40 | Maidenhead | 78 | 75.48 | 86/83 |
| 99.20 | SLOUGH | 82½ | 79.58 | 85 |
| 104.40 | West Drayton | — | 83.38 | 84 |
| 108.55 | Southall | 89½ | 86.36 | 85 |
| 111.95 | Ealing | | | |
| | Broadway | — | 88.55 | 87 |
| 114.90 | Old Oak | | | |
| | Common† | — | 90.59 | 82 |
| 116.40 | Westbourne | | | |
| | Park | 95½ | 92.31 | *40 |
| 117.65 | PADDING- | | | |
| | TON | 100 | 95.33 | — |

* Speed restriction. † New box.
Net time, Bristol-Paddington, 95½min.

working harder. As everyone knows, we failed to achieve the desired 100mph that had been hoped for down the long 1 in 300 falling gradient to Little Somerford. This was due in some small measure to the high wind, for with the valve at 30% cut-off and with full regulator the speed increased to 96mph, and there it stuck, and no more could be got out of it.

"The steam pressure all this time was 220lb/sq in. We had to reduce speed at Wootton Bassett to 60mph to conform with the PW restriction, and we passed there 2 minutes ahead of booked schedule. Swindon was passed in 38 minutes: a distance of 40.5 miles, at 78mph, speed increasing continually: Shrivenham was passed at 82mph, the cut-off being slightly varied to suit the slight variation in the gradient.

"Driver Fred Higby is a most experienced man, he and his firemen were handling the engine beautifully, the steam pressure only varying 10lbs between 220 and 210lb/sq in, the speed range varying between 84 and 86mph. It seems an awful shame that this locomotive, which was running like a sewing machine, should shortly be cut up. It had been decided beforehand that one fireman should fire for the first part of the journey, whilst the other looked after the injectors, the water scoop, and called out the signals to the driver. At Uffington they swapped jobs without a break in the firing rate and they were such good firemen that there was no variation in the steam pressure. Didcot was reached in 54.5 minutes-64.5 miles at an average speed from Swindon to Didcot of 86.5mph.

"As we approached Goring an incident occurred that, had I not been present, I should have found hard to believe — the engine started to prime. That is to say there was so much water in the boiler that it was being pumped out through the chimney. This was amazing seeing that we had been working the engine so hard using 25, 30 and 35% cut off continuously. Anyway, we had to shut off the exhaust injector, and because it was so hot we never got it working properly again, and had to resort to the live steam injector. This reflected on the boiler level, and when it came down to half we had to ease the regulator opening and shorten the travel of the valves. I had planned for us to pass through Reading at 8.00pm and we went through there right on the dot, which was just two minutes before the booked times. Timings were so tight that I was entitled to feel quite satisfied that everything was going to plan. The average speed from Didcot to Reading was 84mph.

"We continued to nurse the engine as much as possible until we had passed Maidenhead, when with 75%

boiler of water, we opened the regulator wide and dropped the lever down to the 30% cut off: the speed being maintained constantly between 80 and 82mph, and in fact passed Old Oak Common at 82mph, only 3 miles from Paddington. We now reduced speed for the restriction through Westbourne Park, finally coming to rest in Paddington at 8.28.5pm-4.5 minutes before our booked time. 117.75 miles in 95.5 minutes from start to stop at an average of 74mph, and in that short time we had consumed approximately 3 tons of coal and 4,000 gallons of water.''

One week later, on 16 May the Oxford University Railway Society used No 5054 *Earl of Ducie* on their own 'Castle Farewell' tour from Paddington to Oxford, Worcester, Hereford and Newport, returning to Paddington via the Severn Tunnel and Reading. *Earl of Ducie* performed admirably on its 325-mile outing with a top speed of 92mph being reached at Honeybourne on the outward journey and again at Little Somerford on the return, with sustained running at speeds of between 75 and 81mph being attained for the whole of the 25 miles between Twyford and Ealing Broadway. Incidentally the University Railway Society minute books show that *Earl of Ducie* cost just £40 to hire for the day.

*Above:*
**No 5050 *Earl of St Germans* stands dead in the yard at Fratton motive power depot on 7 July 1963. It had worked through to Portsmouth with a schools excursion from Parsons Street, Bristol, on 25 June and as 'Castles' were prohibited from Southern lines east of Salisbury it had not been allowed to work home. The three 'Terrier' Class A1X 0-6-0Ts also in shot, Nos 32662, 32646 and 32650 were being prepared for Sunday duties on the Hayling Island branch.** *P. J. Lynch*

*Below:*
**No 5000 *Launceston Castle* receives attention to its fire as it stands on the number one coaling road at Oxford MPD on 27 June 1963.** *D. Tuck*

The 'Castles' undoubtedly went out in style, but it is worth remembering that the performances on these special runs were really no more than what these fine locomotives had been producing day in day out since their introduction in 1923. It is certainly true to say that many of the 'Castles' were withdrawn prematurely and one wonders if it were happening today how British Railways would be able to justify to the taxpayer the cost of fitting four row superheated boilers, double blastpipes and chimneys to 66 locomotives and then to proceed in withdrawing many of them within just a few years. 'Castle' withdrawals had in fact started in 1950

*Above:*
No 4093 *Dunster Castle* leaves Carmarthen with the 1.30pm service to Paddington on 22 April 1963. *A. Doyle*

*Centre right:*
No 7034 *Ince Castle* passes Wolvercote siding, north of Oxford with an up parcels train August 1963. *A. Doyle*

*Bottom right:*
No 5054 *Earl of Ducie* stands at Reading station with the OURS special to Gloucester and Newport on 16 May 1964. *D. Tuck*

with locomotive No 100A1 *Lloyds,* and continued thankfully relatively slowly with only 19 losses up to December 1961. The first true 'Castle' to be withdrawn other than the early rebuilds was No 4091 *Dudley Castle,* being condemned at Old Oak Common on 19 January 1959. It was cut up at Swindon on 21 March of the same year having amassed some 1,691,856 miles in its 34 years of service. In September 1962 No 4037 *The South Wales Borderers* was withdrawn, this 'Star' rebuild had the distinction of attaining the highest mileage of any Great Western locomotive, 776,764 as a 'Star' and a further 1,652,958 as a 'Castle', adding up to a grand total of some 2,429,722 miles. Originally built in December 1910 a quick calculation shows that it ran on average some 57,850 miles per year for each of its 52 years in service. In discussing mileages it is worth noting that no 'Castle' officially reached the two million mile mark, although No 4080 *Powderham Castle* had amassed 1,974,461 miles when recording ceased on 28 December 1963 and may well have broken the two million mark by the time it was finally withdrawn in August 1964. As already mentioned, 1962 proved to be a fateful year for the class as a whole with no less than 55 withdrawals, and this was followed by another 48 in 1963 and 37 in 1964. On 1 January 1963 the Western Region Wolverhampton and Shrewsbury districts were transferred into the London Midland Region Birmingham and Chester divisions respectively. This resulted in a number of 'Castles' being added to the Midland Region book stock. These included the remaining 10 Stafford Road examples Nos 5022/26/ 31/63/89/7001/12/14/19/24/26. Surprisingly they were not all immediately withdrawn by the Midland Region but were reallocated to nearby Oxley after the closure of Stafford Road on 9 September 1963. At Oxley they were used on freight and secondary passenger services in the area. During February 1965 nine of the remaining 13 operational 'Castles' were withdrawn. The four working survivors, Nos 5042 *Winchester Castle,* which incidentally still retained a single chimney, 7022 *Hereford Castle,* 7029 *Clun Castle* and 7034 *Ince Castle* earned their keep in the Gloucester area operating local passenger and freight services. No 5042, 7022 and 7034 were withdrawn in June but No 7029 continued to work on locally, being a regular performer on the 5.45am service from Gloucester to Cardiff and the 5.00pm service from Gloucester Central to Cheltenham St James. *Clun* also proved to be popular for use on special services. It was chosen to haul the last scheduled steam passenger service over the cut-off route, from Paddington to Banbury on 11 June 1965. This was also the last regular 'Castle' class passenger turn from

Paddington, although on 27 November 1965 *Clun Castle* once again visited Paddington to operate the Western Region's last official steam working from the terminus. Its very last official passenger working prior to withdrawal, which of course was also the last scheduled 'Castle' working, took place on 1 January 1966 when it hauled the 5.00pm service from Gloucester to Cheltenham. Interestingly this was not

*Below:*
**No 7009 *Athelney Castle* in ex-works condition, stands outside 'A' shop at Swindon in November 1951.**
*Author's collection*

*Bottom:*
**This interesting picture shows No 4073 *Caerphilly Castle* being prepared for test at Caerphilly works on Monday 19 October 1959. The 'Castle' had just undergone an intermediate repair. 'Castle' repairs were undertaken at Caerphilly from May 1958. It is interesting to speculate whether it received special treatment.** *E. Mountford*

the end of the story for No 7029, for during the same month it was sold to a private buyer and kept in the old Great Western engine shed at Tyseley from where, although no longer a part of the BR fleet, and in private ownership, it saw occasional use on freight services between Bordesley and Banbury yards. Luckily eight members of the class have survived, and of the seven which are still in this country, three are currently operational, thus enabling, as the Great Western so rightly put it, "boys (and girls) of all ages to enjoy the sights and sounds of this most magnificent of machines", the Great Western 'Castle'.

I have included as a footnote this small piece taken from the *Great Western Magazine* of April 1929.

An engineman's young son in a junior class at school was set to form a sentence containing the word 'carefully'. His effort ran thus: "There is a fine engine called the *Carefully Castle*". Enough said!

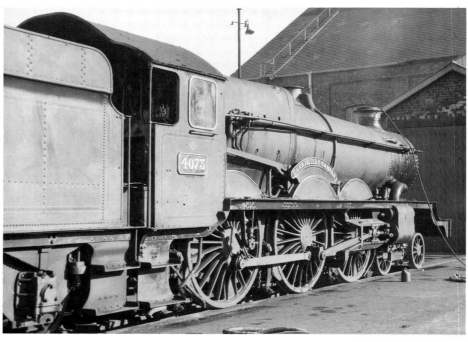

50

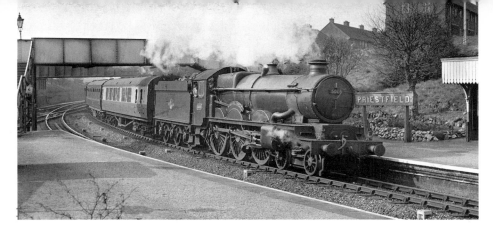

*Left:*
80mph without moving an inch! No 5005 *Manorbier Castle*, newly outshopped, is seen here under test on the rolling road at Swindon testing plant on 4 March 1958. *J. D. Edwards*

*Below left:*
No 7011 *Banbury Castle* is seen here undergoing bogie repairs at Worcester works in November 1964.  *K. C. Farmer*

*Above right:*
No 5008 *Raglan Castle* rounds the sharp curve at Priestfield station with the Saturdays only 4.35pm Wolverhampton-Paddington on 30 April 1960.  *M. Mensing*

*Right:*
No 7014 *Caerhays Castle* piloting No 6015 *King Richard III* near Didcot with the 7.00am up service from Weston-super-Mare on Monday 23 May 1960. At this time, between January and September 1960 the train was double-headed on Mondays, and detached a slip coach and trailer at Didcot. During the rest of the week it was normally hauled by a 'King' alone and slipped only one coach.  *Dr J. Coiley*

*Below:*
The 1.45pm service from Paddington to Cheltenham hauled by No 7000 *Viscount Portal* bursts forth from Sapperton tunnel on 18 June 1960.  *P. J. Kelley*

*Left:*
No 5065 *Bishop's Castle* backs off the traverser at Birmingham Moor Street after arriving with the 1.11pm through service from Portsmouth Harbour on 2 July 1960. *M. Mensing*

*Centre left:*
No 7025 *Sudeley Castle* on the 8.00am service from Kingswear to Liverpool and Manchester negotiates a permanent way slack at Baystonhill south of Shrewsbury on 24 September 1960. This service also carried through coaches for Glasgow. *M. Mensing*

*Bottom:*
No 4085 *Berkeley Castle* is seen here emerging from Snow Hill tunnel with an up parcels service on 12 November 1960. *M. Mensing*

*Above right:*
No 5043 *Earl of Mount Edgcumbe* prepares to leave Cardiff General with the 11.50am service from Swansea to Manchester in June 1961. The locomotive has survived the cutter's torch and is currently in store at Tyseley. *Author's collection*

*Centre right:*
No 5059 *Earl St Aldwyn* leaves Weston-super-Mare on 15 June 1961 with a through service to the Midlands. The long gone excursion station at Locking Road can be seen on the right. *E. T. Gill*

*Bottom right:*
A regular ex-Swindon running-in turn was the 3.35pm fish empties from Swindon to Hull and Grimsby. The ex-works locomotive worked as far as Banbury. 'Castles' made regular appearances on this duty and on a lovely summer evening, No 4074 *Caldicot Castle* is seen approaching Oxford 24 June 1961. *W. J. Turner*

*Above left:*
A very clean No 5001 *Llandovery Castle* enters Worcester Shrub Hill on 17 August 1961 with the Hereford portion of the up 'Cathedrals Express'. Here extra coaches will be added prior to its departure for Paddington. *G. D. King*

*Left:*
A group of youthful 'spotters' eagerly await the departure of No 5022 *Wigmore Castle* with the 4.10pm service to Paddington from Wolverhampton (Low Level) on 1 September 1961. *Dr G. Smith*

*Below left:*
No 4075 *Cardiff Castle* speeds past Milton, west of Didcot with the 11.55am Paddington-Pembroke Dock/Milford Haven service on 22 September 1961. *M. Mensing*

*Top:*
No 5078 *Beaufort* as rebuilt with a double chimney accelerates past Southall gas works on Saturday 23 December 1961 with the down 'Pembroke Coast Express'. *M. Pope*

*Right:*
No 5087 *Tintern Abbey* pulls away from Badminton with a Paddington-Cardiff service on 13 April 1962. *G. A. Richardson*

*Left:*
Llanelly-allocated 'Castles' were rare visitors to Oxford. Here on a sunny day in June 1962 No 5016 *Montgomery Castle* pulls away with a Saturday extra from the Midlands to the South Coast. *W. Turner*

*Bottom left:*
A Swindon-Paddington stopping service calls at Didcot on 6 June 1962. The locomotive, No 7037 *Swindon*, was the last 'Castle' to be constructed at Swindon works. *D. Tuck*

*Bottom:*
No 5025 *Chirk Castle* of Oxford shed takes the up relief line at Kennington Junction with an express freight service from Hinksey Yards to Reading and Basingstoke in summer 1962. *A. Simpkins*

*Above right:*
No 7032 *Denbigh Castle*, banked by 2-6-2T No 6113, emerges from Whiteball tunnel with a lengthy relief to the 7.30am Paddington-Penzance service on 4 August 1962. *M. J. Fox*

*Right:*
The summer of 1962 was the last summer in which steam commanded the bulk of the expresses from Paddington. On a hot, sunny, August day No 7022 *Hereford Castle* passes West Ealing on a down express on 25 August 1962.
*Dr D. P. Williams*

*Bottom right:*
The afternoon sun shines through a cloudless sky as No 5076 *Gladiator* passes Kidlington box with the 8.42am Shrewsbury-Paddington parcels in August 1962. *A. Simpkins*

**Left:**
No 5060 *Earl of Berkeley* passes the Kennet & Avon pumping station at Crofton, near Savernake with a down West of England relief service on Saturday 22 September 1962. *M. Pope*

**Centre left:**
No 7008 *Swansea Castle* receives admiring glances from a group of young spotters as it backs its train of empty stock from the 2.38pm Oxford service away to Old Oak Common carriage sidings on 6 April 1963. Apart from its last year in service, *Swansea Castle* spent almost the whole of its working life at Oxford, being delivered from new in March 1948. It was reallocated to Old Oak Common in April 1963 and withdrawn from service in October 1964. *D. Tuck*

**Below:**
Reading (81D) allocated No 5018 *St Mawes Castle* prepares to leave Exeter St Davids with the 8.30am service from Paddington to Penzance on 1 June 1963. *Author's collection.*

**Top right:**
A fine portrait of No 5085 *Evesham Abbey* as it receives attention at Oxford MPD on 9 June 1963. *D. Tuck*

**Centre right:**
A through service to Shrewsbury prepares to leave Cardiff General hauled by No 4093 *Dunster Castle* June 1963. *Author's collection*

**Below right:**
No 5057 *Earl Waldegrave* being turned at Newbury Racecourse during the final day of steam operations on the Newbury race specials, Saturday 27 July 1963. *D. Tuck*

**Left**
Driver Newton of Old Oak Common proudly stands alongside No 7029 *Clun Castle* after arrival at Newbury Racecourse with a race special from Paddington on the last occasion that steam was used on the specials. *D. Tuck*

**Above:**
No 5054 *Earl of Ducie* stands under the roof at Paddington on 9 May 1964 after arriving with the Ian Allan high speed special from Plymouth via Bristol. The special commemorated the epic run made in 1904 by *City of Truro*. On this occasion *Earl of Ducie* just failed to top the three figure mark, reaching a top speed of 96mph near Little Somerford.
*B. Stephenson*

**Centre right:**
No 4037 *The South Wales Borderers*, seen here entering Colwall tunnel with a Paddington-Hereford service, started life in December 1910 as 'Star' class *Queen Philippa*. It was rebuilt as a 'Castle' in June 1926, and subsequently renamed *The South Wales Borderers* in March 1937. It was withdrawn from service in September 1962, having amassed some 2,429,722 miles in service an all time record for any ex-Great Western locomotive. *M. Mensing*

**Right:**
A rather run-down and grubby No 7008 *Swansea Castle* arrives at Banbury on 27 June 1964 with a through summer service from the Midlands to the South Coast. *D. Tuck*

*Above left:*
Relegated to secondary duties, No 7005 *Sir Edward Elgar*, fitted with what appears to be a wooden smokebox number plate, rounds Hatton North triangle with the 7.45pm service from Evesham to Birmingham on 4 July 1964. No 7005 is just two months away from withdrawal. *P. Riley*

*Above right:*
The last scheduled 'Castle'-hauled service from Paddington was the 4.15pm stopping service to Banbury via Bicester. Here No 7022 *Hereford Castle*, devoid of all name and numberplates and in appalling external condition, prepares to leave Princes Risborough for Banbury on 13 April 1965. *D. Tuck*

*Left:*
The final scheduled steam-hauled passenger service from Paddington, the 4.15pm service to Banbury, is seen here leaving Paddington on Friday 11 June 1965 hauled by No 7029 *Clun Castle*. Note the bugle player, probably sounding the last post. *Great Western Trust*

*Below:*
Although privately owned, No 7029 *Clun Castle* still earned its keep working on a variety of services in the West Midlands. Here on 23 May 1967 it tops Hatton bank with the 12.10pm Banbury-Bordesley freight. No 7029 had actually been withdrawn from Western Region operating stock on 31 December 1965. *P. Riley*

# Appendix One

## OURS SURVEY 13 JUNE 1959

The following table is taken from a daytime traffic survey in the Thames Valley area, undertaken by the Oxford University Railway Society between approximately 6.00am and 6.00pm on Saturday 13 June 1959. Although some of the services were at this time diesel hauled the majority were still steam operated. The table below gives some indication of 'Castle' Class workings on main line services in and out of Paddington.

Down Departures from Paddington.

| Dep | Destination | Locomotive | Shed | Load |
|---|---|---|---|---|
| 5.55am | Carmarthen (i) | 7001 *Sir James Milne* | 81A | 13 |
| 6.05am | Oxford | 5025 *Chirk Castle* | 81F | 13 |
| 8.40am | Pembroke Dock | 4074 *Caldicot Castle* | 87E | 9 |
| 9.03am | Newquay | 5021 *Whittington Castle* | 83D | 12 |
| 9.20am | Paignton | 7004 *Eastnor Castle* | 81A | 11 |
| 9.45am | Hereford | 7032 *Denbigh Castle* | 81A | 13 |
| 10.05am | Taunton | 5064 *Bishop's Castle* | 82C | 11 |
| 10.55am | Pembroke Dock (ii) | 5091 *Cleeve Abbey* | 87E | 13 |
| 11.05am | Cheltenham | 5044 *Earl of Dunraven* | 81A | 8 |
| 11.30am | Penzance | 5082 *Swordfish* | 81A | 10 |
| 11.45am | Hereford | 5042 *Winchester Castle* | 85A | 10 |
| 11.55am | Pembroke Dock | 5016 *Montgomery Castle* | 87E | 11 |
| 12.00 | Kingswear (iii) | 4098 *Kidwelly Castle* | 83A | 13 |
| 12.25pm | Reading | 5010 *Restormel Castle* | 81D | 5 |
| 1.15pm | Weston-super-Mare | 5085 *Evesham Abbey* | 82A | 9 |
| 1.24pm | Swindon | 5065 *Newport Castle* | 81A | 5 |
| 1.45pm | Hereford | 5037 *Monmouth Castle* | 85A | 13 |
| 1.50pm | Carmarthen | 4096 *Highclere Castle* | 81A | 12 |
| 2.15pm | Cheltenham | 5094 *Tretower Castle* | 85B | 10+1van |
| 2.21pm | Plymouth parcels | 4085 *Berkeley Castle* | 85B | 24v |
| 4.15pm | Plymouth | 4082 *Windsor Castle* | 81A | 10+1van |
| 4.38pm | Worcester | 7007 *Great Western* | 85A | 9 |
| 4.45pm | Hereford (iv) | 7005 *Sir Edward Elgar* | 85A | 11 |
| 4.55pm | Cheltenham (v) | 7000 *Viscount Portal* | 85B | 8 |
| 5.00pm | Weston-super-Mare | 5090 *Neath Abbey* | 82A | 8 |

The last regular Class 1 passenger turns for the 'Castles' were on the Paddington-Worcester services. The following photographs illustrate the final months of these workings and are included as a fitting tribute to the class.

*Below:*
No 7034 *Ince Castle*, in rather grubby condition, stands at Platform 6 at Paddington after arriving with the up 'Cathedrals Express' on Saturday 6 April 1963. *Dr G. Smith*

Up Trains listed in order of arrival.

| Dep | From | Locomotive | Shed | Load |
|---|---|---|---|---|
| 6.30am | Worcester | 5042 *Winchester Castle* | 85A | 7 |
| 8.00am | Cheltenham(v) | 5094 *Tretower Castle* | 85B | 9 |
| 6.15am | Swansea | 4096 *Highclere Castle* | 81A | 12 |
| excursion | Parson Street | 5005 *Manorbier Castle* | 82C | 9 |
| excursion | Bilston | 5072 *Hurricane* | 84A | 11 |
| excursion | Wolverhampton | 5019 *Treago Castle* | 84A | 9 |
| 8.30am | Bristol | 5057 *Earl Waldegrave* | 82A | 11 |
| 8.20am | Weston-super-Mare | 5085 *Evesham Abbey* | 82A | 10 |
| 7.45 am | Hereford (iv) | 5037 *Monmouth Castle* | 85A | 11 |
| 4.55 am | Fishguard | 5035 *Coity Castle* | 81A | 12 |
| excursion | Treherbert | 7025 *Sudeley Castle* | 81A | 8 |
| 7.50am | Taunton | 4085 *Berkeley Castle* | 85B | 8 |
| 8.40am | Paignton | 4080 *Powderham Castle* | 83A | 9 |
| 11.45am | Bristol | 5090 *Neath Abbey* | 82A | 9 |
| 12.45pm | Oxford | 5025 *Chirk Castle* | 81F | 9 |
| 10.05am | Paignton | 5011 *Tintagel Castle* | 83A | 10 |
| 12.55pm | Didcot | 7007 *Great Western* | 85A | 8 |
| 11.45am | Cheltenham | 7000 *Viscount Portal* | 85B | 10 |
| 10.58am | Paignton | 5024 *Carew Castle* | 83A | 11 |
| 11.15am | Hereford | 7005 *Sir Edward Elgar* | 85A | 10 |
| 11.23am | Churston | 5003 *Lulworth Castle* | 83A | 12 |
| 11.25am | Kingswear (iii) | 5066 *Sir Felix Pole* | 81A | 10 |
| 9.00am | Neyland | 5095 *Barbury Castle* | 86C | 11 |
| 12.55pm | Hereford | 4088 *Dartmouth Castle* | 85A | 9 |
| 5.15pm | Windsor | 5088 *Llanthony Abbey* | 84A | 10 |
| 4.18pm | Swindon | 7027 *Thornbury Castle* | 81A | 4+1van |
| 11.10am | Milford Haven | 5056 *Earl of Powis* | 81A | 11 |
| 2.15pm | Wolverhampton | 7032 *Denbigh Castle* | 81A | 6 |
| 2.00pm | Paignton | 4077 *Chepstow Castle* | 83A | 10 |
| 10.35pm | Plymouth | 7031 *Cromwell's Castle* | 83D | 9 |
| 4.00pm | Cheltenham | 5044 *Earl of Dunraven* | 81A | 8 |

| (i) | The 'Red Dragon' |
|---|---|
| (ii) | 'Pembroke Coast Express' |
| (iii) | 'Torbay Express' |
| (iv) | 'Cathedrals Express' |
| (v) | 'Cheltenham Spa Express'. |

*Below:*
**No 7025 *Sudeley Castle* pulls away from Oxford with the 9.50am service from Hereford to Paddington, the 'Cathedrals Express' in May 1963.** *Dr. G. Smith*

Other 'Castle' class workings noted during the survey:

Down

| Service | | Locomotive | Shed | Load |
|---------|---|------------|------|------|
| 8.55am | Ramsgate-Birkenhead | 5061 *Earl of Birkenhead* + | 81D | 11 |
| 9.33am | Bournemouth-Birkenhead | 7008 *Swansea Castle** | 81F | 12 |
| 10.54am | Swindon- Gloucester | 5023 *Brecon Castle* | 82C | 6 |
| 1.02pm | Swindon-Taunton | 4079 *Pendennis Castle* | 82C | 7+2vans |

Up

| Service | | Locomotive | Shed | Load |
|---------|---|------------|------|------|
| 7.35am | Birkenhead-Margate | 5022 *Wigmore Castle* x | 84A | 14 |
| 8.50am | Cheltenham-Swindon | 4085 *Berkeley Castle* | 85B | 5+2vans |
| 10.20am | Swindon-Reading | 5065 *Newport Castle* | 81A | 2 |
| 11.45am | Oxford-Didcot | 7007 *Great Western* | 85A | 7 |
| 1155am | Swindon-Didcot | 5008 *Raglan Castle* | 81A | 4 |
| 2.40pm | Gloucester-Swindon | 5023 *Brecon Castle* | 82C | 7 |
| 4.15pm | Chippenham-Swindon | 5064 *Bishop's Castle* | 82C | 4 |

\* from Oxford
+ from Reading
x to Reading

A total of 67 services seen, using 49 different locomotives.

**Below:**
No 7007 *Great Western* crosses the Rewley Abbey stream as it leaves Oxford with an afternoon service to Worcester.
*J. D. Edwards*

**Top right:**
On a rather misty February day, No 5057 *Earl Waldegrave* accelerates away past Wolvercote Siding box, north of Oxford, with the 11.15am service from Paddington to Worcester on 26 February 1963.
*Dr. G. Smith*

**Centre right:**
The 11.10am service from Worcester to Paddington is seen here at speed near Combe on Friday 1 March 1963 hauled by No 7023 *Penrice Castle*. This locomotive worked the last official steam-hauled service from Worcester to Paddington on Saturday 7 September 1963. *Dr G. Smith*

**Bottom right:**
The Cotswold village of Stonesfield makes a fine backdrop as an unidentified 'Castle' heads through the Evenlode valley with the 11.10am service from Worcester on 19 December 1962. *Dr G. Smith*

*Left:*
No 7003 *Elmley Castle* of Gloucester shed makes a dramatic sight as it attacks Chipping Camden bank with the 1.10pm service from Worcester to Paddington on 2 March 1963.  *Dr G. Smith*

*Below:*
The steepest stretch on the Cotswold line is the six miles of 1 in 100 climb from Honeybourne to Campden. Here on Saturday 25 May 1963 No 7025 *Sudeley Castle* powers its way up the bank with the 11.10am service from Worcester to Paddington.  *Dr G. Smith*

*Bottom:*
No 7023 *Penrice Castle* simmers gently at Paddington on Saturday 7 September 1963 after arriving with the 11.10am service from Worcester, the last scheduled 'Castle' working on Paddington-Worcester passenger services.  *D. Tuck*

# **A**ppendix Two

## CONSTRUCTION AND WITHDRAWAL OF 'CASTLE' CLASS

|  | Date Built | Double Chimney | Date Withdrawn | Final Mileage |
|---|---|---|---|---|
| 100 Al *Lloyds* | 4/25* |  | 3/50 | 1,164,297 |
| 111 *Viscount Churchill* | 9/24# |  | 7/53 | 1,426,356* |
| 4000 *North Star* | 11/29* |  | 5/57 | 1,191,592* |
| 4000 *North Star* | 11/29* |  | 5/57 | 1,191,592* |
| 4016 *The Somerset Light Infantry (Prince Albert's)* | 10/25* |  | 9/51 | 1,186,663* |
| 4032 *Queen Alexandra* | 4/26* |  | 9/51 | 1,225,908* |
| 4037 *The South Wales Borderers* | 6/26* |  | 9/62 | 1,652,958* |
| 4073 *Caerphilly Castle* | 8/23 |  | 5/60 | 1,910,730 |
| 4074 *Caldicot Castle* | 12/23 | 4/59 | 5/63 | 1,844,072 |
| 4075 *Cardiff Castle* | 1/24 |  | 11/61 | 1,807,802 |
| 4076 *Carmarthen Castle* | 2/24 |  | 2/63 | 1,697,895 |
| 4077 *Chepstow Castle* | 2/24 |  | 8/62 | 1,823,488 |
| 4078 *Pembroke Castle* | 2/24 |  | 7/62 | 1,917,380 |
| 4079 *Pendennis Castle* | 2/24 |  | 5/64 | 1,758,398 |
| 4080 *Powderham Castle* | 3/24 | 8/58 | 8/64 | 1,974,461 |
| 4081 *Warwick Castle* | 3/24 |  | 1/63 | 1,894,998 |
| 4082 *Windsor Castle* | 4/24 |  | 9/64 | 1,898,571 |
| 4083 *Abbotsbury Castle* | 5/25 |  | 12/61 | 1,677,060 |
| 4084 *Aberystwyth Castle* | 5/25 |  | 10/60 | 1,674,812 |
| 4085 *Berkeley Castle* | 5/25 |  | 5/62 | 1,651,000 |
| 4086 *Builth Castle* | 6/25 |  | 4/62 | 1,791,633 |
| 4087 *Cardigan Castle* | 6/25 | 2/58 | 10/63 | 1,812,341 |
| 4088 *Dartmouth Castle* | 7/25 | 5/58 | 5/64 | 1,848,430 |
| 4089 *Donnington Castle* | 7/25 |  | 9/64 | 1,876,807 |
| 4090 *Dorchester Castle* | 7/25 | 4/57 | 6/63 | 1,848,646 |
| 4091 *Dudley Castle* | 7/25 |  | 1/59 | 1,691,856 |
| 4092 *Dunraven Castle* | 8/25 |  | 12/61 | 1,718,879 |
| 4093 *Dunster Castle* | 5/26 | 12/57 | 9/64 | 1,842,985 |
| 4094 *Dynevor Castle* | 5/26 |  | 3/62 | 1,881,886 |
| 4095 *Harlech Castle* | 6/26 |  | 12/62 | 1,695,899 |
| 4096 *Highclere Castle* | 6/26 |  | 1/63 | 1,958,378 |
| 4097 *Kenilworth Castle* | 6/26 | 6/58 | 5/60 | 1,713,996 |
| 4098 *Kidwelly Castle* | 7/26 |  | 12/63 | 1,723,879 |
| 4099 *Kilgerran Castle* | 8/26 |  | 9/62 | 1,873,985 |
| 5000 *Launceston Castle* | 9/26 |  | 10/64 | 1,870,200 |
| 5001 *Llandovery Castle* | 9/26 | 7/61 | 2/63 | 1,855,495 |
| 5002 *Ludlow Castle* | 9/26 |  | 9/64 | 1,817,218 |
| 5003 *Lulworth Castle* | 5/27 |  | 8/62 | 1,698,751 |
| 5004 *Llanstephan Castle* | 6/27 |  | 4/62 | 1,854,704 |
| 5005 *Manorbier Castle* | 6/27 |  | 2/60 | 1,731,868 |
| 5006 *Tregenna Castle* | 6/27 |  | 4/62 | 1,812,966 |
| 5007 *Rougemont Castle* | 6/27 |  | 9/62 | 1,854,951 |
| 5008 *Raglan Castle* | 6/27 | 3/61 | 9/62 | 1,798,646 |
| 5009 *Shrewsbury Castle* | 6/27 |  | 10/60 | 1,708,246 |
| 5010 *Restormel Castle* | 7/27 |  | 10/59 | 1,684,146 |
| 5011 *Tintagel Castle* | 7/27 |  | 9/62 | 1,732,565 |
| 5012 *Berry Pomeroy Castle* | 7/27 |  | 4/62 | 1,625,955 |
| 5013 *Abergavenny Castle* | 6/32 |  | 7/62 | 1,525,662 |
| 5014 *Goodrich Castle* | 6/32 |  | 2/65 | 1,615,297 |
| 5015 *Kingswear Castle* | 7/32 |  | 4/63 | 1,554,288 |
| 5016 *Montgomery Castle* | 7/32 | 2/61 | 9/62 | 1,480,896 |
| 5017 *The Gloucestershire Regiment 28th/61st* | 7/32 |  | 9/62 | 1,598,851 |

*Below:*
**Nameplate of No 4016 *The Somerset Light Infantry (Prince Albert's).*
Authors's collection**

*Below:*
**Nameplate of No 4037 *The South Wales Borderers.* Author's collection**

| | Date Built | Double Chimney | Date Withdrawn | Final Mileage |
|---|---|---|---|---|
| 5018 *St Mawes Castle* | 7/32 | | 3/64 | 1,503,642 |
| 5019 *Treago Castle* | 7/32 | 3/61 | 9/62 | 1,521,335 |
| 5020 *Trematon Castle* | 7/32 | | 11/62 | 1,636,799 |
| 5021 *Whittington Castle* | 8/32 | | 9/62 | 1,446,986 |
| 5022 *Wigmore Castle* | 8/32 | 2/59 | 6/63 | 1,546,104 |
| 5023 *Brecon Castle* | 4/34 | | 2/63 | 1,479,168 |
| 5024 *Carew Castle* | 4/34 | | 5/62 | 1,351,161 |
| 5025 *Chirk Castle* | 4/34 | | 11/63 | 1,401,530 |
| 5026 *Criccieth Castle* | 4/34 | 10/59 | 11/64 | 1,209,457 |
| 5027 *Farleigh Castle* | 4/34 | 4/61 | 11/62 | 1,465,365 |
| 5028 *Llantilio Castle* | 5/34 | | 5/60 | 1,345,291 |
| 5029 *Nunney Castle* | 5/34 | | 12/63 | 1,523,415 |
| 5030 *Shirburn Castle* | 5/34 | | 9/62 | 1,413,084 |
| 5031 *Totnes Castle* | 5/34 | 6/59 | 10/63 | 1,434,409 |
| 5032 *Usk Castle* | 5/34 | 5/59 | 9/62 | 1,288,968 |
| 5033 *Broughton Castle* | 5/35 | 10/60 | 9/62 | 1,160,197 |
| 5034 *Corfe Castle* | 5/35 | 2/61 | 9/62 | 1,250,714 |
| 5035 *Coity Castle* | 5/35 | | 5/62 | 1,444,261 |
| 5036 *Lyonshall Castle* | 5/35 | 12/60 | 9/62 | 1,304,430 |
| 5037 *Monmouth Castle* | 5/35 | | 3/64 | 1,500,851 |
| 5038 *Morlais Castle* | 6/35 | | 9/63 | 1,438,862 |
| 5039 *Rhuddlan Castle* | 6/35 | | 6/64 | 1,380,564 |
| 5040 *Stokesay Castle* | 6/35 | | 10/63 | 1,414,142 |
| 5041 *Tiverton Castle* | 7/35 | | 12/63 | 1,383,804 |
| 5042 *Winchester Castle* | 7/35 | | 6/65 | 1,339,221 |
| 5043 *Earl of Mount Edgcumbe* | 3/36 | 5/58 | 12/63 | 1,400,817 |
| 5044 *Earl of Dunraven* | 3/36 | | 4/62 | 1,377,646 |
| 5045 *Earl of Dudley* | 3/36 | | 9/62 | 1,383,737 |
| 5046 *Earl Cawdor* | 4/36 | | 9/62 | 1,358,388 |
| 5047 *Earl of Dartmouth* | 4/36 | | 9/62 | 1,225,670 |
| 5048 *Earl of Devon* | 4/36 | | 8/62 | 1,327,811 |
| 5049 *Earl of Plymouth* | 4/36 | 9/59 | 3/63 | 1,282,965 |
| 5050 *Earl of St Germans* | 5/36 | | 8/63 | 1,135,797 |
| 5051 *Earl Bathurst* | 5/36 | | 5/63 | 1,316,659 |
| 5052 *Earl of Radnor* | 5/36 | | 9/62 | 1,396,894 |
| 5053 *Earl Cairns* | 5/36 | | 7/62 | 1,293,786 |
| 5054 *Earl of Ducie* | 6/36 | | 10/64 | 1,412,394 |
| 5055 *Earl of Eldon* | 6/36 | | 9/64 | 1,439,975 |
| 5056 *Earl of Powis* | 6/36 | 11/60 | 11/64 | 1,434,833 |
| 5057 *Earl Waldegrave* | 6/36 | 5/58 | 3/64 | 1,273,324 |
| 5058 *Earl of Clancarty* | 5/37 | | 3/63 | 1,224,735 |
| 5059 *Earl St Aldwyn* | 5/37 | | 6/62 | 1,054,602 |
| 5060 *Earl of Berkeley* | 6/37 | 8/61 | 4/63 | 1,316,240 |
| 5061 *Earl of Birkenhead* | 6/37 | 9/58 | 9/62 | 1,020,412 |
| 5062 *Earl of Shaftesbury* | 6/37 | | 8/62 | 1,143,143 |
| 5063 *Earl Baldwin* | 6/37 | | 2/65 | 1,267,425 |
| 5064 *Bishop's Castle* | 6/37 | 9/58 | 6/62 | 1,155,986 |
| 5065 *Newport Castle* | 7/37 | | 1/63 | 1,222,961 |
| 5066 *Sir Felix Pole* | 7/37 | 4/59 | 9/62 | 1,339,619 |
| 5067 *St Fagans Castle* | 8/37 | | 7/62 | 1,192,663 |
| 5068 *Beverston Castle* | 6/38 | 3/61 | 9/62 | 1,081,514 |
| 5069 *Isambard Kingdom Brunel* | 6/38 | 11/58 | 2/62 | 1,217,505 |
| 5070 *Sir Daniel Gooch* | 6/38 | | 3/64 | 1,139,354 |
| 5071 *Spitfire* | 6/38 | 6/59 | 10/63 | 1,150,913 |
| 5072 *Hurricane* | 6/38 | | 10/62 | 1,055,942 |
| 5073 *Blenheim* | 7/38 | 7/59 | 2/64 | 995,495 |
| 5074 *Hampden* | 7/38 | 9/61 | 5/64 | 1,142,187 |
| 5075 *Wellington* | 8/38 | | 9/62 | 1,068,502 |
| 5076 *Gladiator* | 8/38 | | 9/64 | 1,121,080 |
| 5077 *Fairey Battle* | 8/38 | | 7/62 | 1,089,166 |
| 5078 *Beaufort* | 5/39 | 12/61 | 11/62 | 1,038,165 |
| 5079 *Lysander* | 5/39 | | 5/60 | 1,008,175 |
| 5080 *Defiant* | 5/39 | | 4/63 | 1,117,030 |
| 5081 *Lockheed Hudson* | 5/39 | | 10/63 | 1,208,003 |
| 5082 *Swordfish* | 6/39 | | 7/62 | 1,161,413 |
| 5083 *Bath Abbey* | 6/39* | | 1/59 | 1,001,686 |
| 5084 *Reading Abbey* | 4/37* | 10/58 | 7/62 | 1,188,386 |
| 5085 *Evesham Abbey* | 7/39* | | 2/64 | 1,214,357 |
| 5086 *Viscount Horne* | 12/37* | | 11/58 | 1,060,724 |

**Below:**
Nameplate of No 5012 *Berry Pomeroy Castle. Author's collection*

|  | Date Built | Double Chimney | Date Withdrawn | Final Mileage |
|---|---|---|---|---|
| 5087 *Tintern Abbey* | 11/40* |  | 8/63 | 1,088,932 |
| 5088 *Llanthony Abbey* | 2/39* | 6/58 | 9/62 | 1,047,102 |
| 5089 *Westminster Abbey* | 10/39* |  | 11/64 | 1,158,893 |
| 5090 *Neath Abbey* | 4/39* |  | 5/62 | 1,161,961 |
| 5091 *Cleeve Abbey* | 12/38* |  | 10/64 | 1,082,935 |
| 5092 *Tresco Abbey* | 4/38* | 10/61 | 7/63 | 1,143,594 |
| 5093 *Upton Castle* | 6/39 |  | 9/63 | 1,145,221 |
| 5094 *Tretower Castle* | 6/39 | 6/60 | 9/62 | 948,540 |
| 5095 *Barbury Castle* | 6/39 | 11/58 | 8/62 | 1,122,493 |
| 5096 *Bridgwater Castle* | 6/39 |  | 6/64 | 1,103,607 |
| 5097 *Sarum Castle* | 6/39 | 7/61 | 3/63 | 993,804 |
| 5098 *Clifford Castle* | 5/46 | 1/59 | 6/64 | 826,525 |
| 5099 *Compton Castle* | 5/46 |  | 2/63 | 863,411 |
| 7000 *Viscount Portal* | 5/46 |  | 12/63 | 824,873 |
| 7001 *Sir James Milne* | 5/46 | 9/60 | 9/63 | 838,604 |
| 7002 *Devizes Castle* | 6/46 | 7/61 | 3/64 | 837,626 |
| 7003 *Elmley Castle* | 6/46 | 6/60 | 8/64 | 773,642 |
| 7004 *Eastnor Castle* | 6/46 | 2/58 | 1/64 | 876,349 |
| 7005 *Sir Edward Elgar* | 6/46 |  | 9/64 | 869,370 |
| 7006 *Lydford Castle* | 6/46 | 6/60 | 12/63 | 789,052 |
| 7007 *Great Western* | 7/46 | 6/61 | 2/63 | 851,649 |
| 7008 *Swansea Castle* | 5/48 | 6/59 | 9/64 | 483,663 |
| 7009 *Athelney Castle* | 5/48 |  | 3/63 | 671,920 |
| 7010 *Avondale Castle* | 6/48 | 10/60 | 3/64 | 669,192 |
| 7011 *Banbury Castle* | 6/48 |  | 2/65 | 748,635 |
| 7012 *Barry Castle* | 6/48 |  | 11/64 | 667,408 |
| 7013 *Bristol Castle* | 7/48 | 5/58 | 2/65 | 712,286 |
| 7014 *Caerhays Castle* | 7/48 | 2/59 | 2/65 | 765,282 |
| 7015 *Carn Brea Castle* | 7/48 | 5/59 | 4/63 | 636,439 |
| 7016 *Chester Castle* | 8/48 |  | 11/62 | 672,533 |
| 7017 *G. J. Churchward* | 8/48 |  | 2/63 | 724,589 |
| 7018 *Drysllwyn Castle* | 5/49 | 5/56 | 9/63 | 614,259 |
| 7019 *Fowey Castle* | 5/49 | 9/58 | 2/65 | 680,454 |
| 7020 *Gloucester Castle* | 5/49 | 2/61 | 9/64 | 610,143 |
| 7021 *Haverfordwest Castle* | 6/49 | 11/61 | 9/63 | 673,231 |
| 7022 *Hereford Castle* | 6/49 | 1/58 | 6/65 | 733,069 |
| 7023 *Penrice Castle* | 6/49 | 5/58 | 2/65 | 730,636 |
| 7024 *Powis Castle* | 6/49 | 3/59 | 2/65 | 731,344 |
| 7025 *Sudeley Castle* | 8/49 |  | 9/64 | 685,916 |
| 7026 *Tenby Castle* | 8/49 |  | 10/64 | 636,668 |
| 7027 *Thornbury Castle* | 8/49 |  | 12/63 | 728,843 |
| 7028 *Cadbury Castle* | 5/50 | 10/61 | 12/63 | 624,626 |
| 7029 *Clun Castle* | 5/50 | 10/59 | 12/65 | 618,073 |
| 7030 *Cranbrook Castle* | 6/50 | 7/59 | 2/63 | 637,339 |
| 7031 *Cromwell's Castle* | 6/50 |  | 7/63 | 749,715 |
| 7032 *Denbigh Castle* | 6/50 | 9/60 | 9/64 | 666,374 |
| 7033 *Hartlebury Castle* | 7/50 | 7/59 | 1/63 | 605,219 |
| 7034 *Ince Castle* | 8/50 | 12/59 | 6/65 | 616,584 |
| 7035 *Ogmore Castle* | 8/50 | 1/60 | 6/64 | 580,346 |
| 7036 *Taunton Castle* | 8/50 | 8/59 | 9/63 | 617,653 |
| 7037 *Swindon* | 8/50 |  | 3/63 | 519,885 |

Names have been listed as carried on withdrawal. Mileage records are correct to 28 December 1963, after which recording ceased. Rebuilt engine mileages are as 'Castle' class only and are denoted thus *

*Below:*
**Nameplate of No 5069, the longest of the class, *Isambard Kingdom Brunel*.**
**Author's collection**

#Rebuilt from 4-6-2 *The Great Bear*.
*Rebuilt from 'Star' class.

Number constructed/rebuilt per year.

| | | | |
|---|---|---|---|
| 1923 | 2 | 1936 | 15 |
| 1924 | 8 + 1R | 1937 | 10 + 2R |
| 1925 | 10 + 2R | 1938 | 10 + 2R |
| 1926 | 10 + 2R | 1939 | 10 + 5R |
| 1927 | 10 | 1948 | 10 |
| 1929 | 1R | 1949 | 10 |
| 1932 | 10 | 1950 | 10 |
| 1935 | 10 | Total | 171 |

# Appendix Three

## CHANGES OF NAME

| First Name | New Name | Date |
|---|---|---|
| 4009 *Shooting Star* | *Lloyds* | 1/36* |
| 4016 *Knight of the Golden Fleece* | *The Somerset Light Infantry (Prince Albert's)* | 1/38 |
| 4037 *Queen Phillipa* | *The South Wales Borderers* | 3/37 |
| 5017 *St Donat's Castle* | *The Gloucestershire Regiment 28th/61st* | 4/54 |
| 5043 *Barbury Castle* | *Earl of Mount Edgcumbe* | 9/37 |
| 5044 *Beverston Castle* | *Earl of Dunraven* | 9/37 |
| 5045 *Bridgwater Castle* | *Earl of Dudley* | 9/37 |
| 5046 *Clifford Castle* | *Earl Cawdor* | 8/37 |
| 5047 *Compton Castle* | *Earl of Dartmouth* | 8/37 |
| 5048 *Cranbrook Castle* | *Earl of Devon* | 8/37 |
| 5049 *Denbigh Castle* | *Earl of Plymouth* | 8/37 |
| 5050 *Devizes Castle* | *Earl of St Germans* | 8/37 |
| 5051 *Drysllwyn Castle* | *Earl Bathurst* | 8/37 |
| 5052 *Eastnor Castle* | *Earl of Radnor* | 7/37 |
| 5053 *Bishop's Castle* | *Earl Cairns* | 8/37 |
| 5054 *Lamphey Castle* | *Earl of Ducie* | 9/37 |
| 5055 *Lydford Castle* | *Earl of Eldon* | 8/37 |
| 5056 *Ogmore Castle* | *Earl of Powis* | 9/37 |
| 5057 *Penrice Castle* | *Earl Waldegrave* | 10/37 |
| 5058 *Newport Castle* | *Earl of Clancarty* | 9/37 |
| 5059 *Powis Castle* | *Earl St Aldwyn* | 10/37 |
| 5060 *Sarum Castle* | *Earl of Berkeley* | 10/37 |
| 5061 *Sudeley Castle* | *Earl of Birkenhead* | 10/37 |
| 5062 *Tenby Castle* | *Earl of Shaftesbury* | 11/37 |
| 5063 *Thornbury Castle* | *Earl Baldwin* | 7/37 |
| 5064 *Tretower Castle* | *Bishop's Castle* | 9/37 |
| 5065 *Upton Castle* | *Newport Castle* | 9/37 |
| 5066 *Wardour Castle* | *Sir Felix Pole* | 4/56 |
| 5071 *Clifford Castle* | *Spitfire* | 9/40 |
| 5072 *Compton Castle* | *Hurricane* | 11/40 |
| 5073 *Cranbrook Castle* | *Blenheim* | 1/41 |
| 5074 *Denbigh Castle* | *Hampden* | 1/41 |
| 5075 *Devizes Castle* | *Wellington* | 10/40 |
| 5076 *Drysllwyn Castle* | *Gladiator* | 1/41 |
| 5077 *Eastnor Castle* | *Fairey Battle* | 10/40 |
| 5078 *Lamphey Castle* | *Beaufort* | 1/41 |
| 5079 *Lydford Castle* | *Lysander* | 11/40 |
| 5080 *Ogmore Castle* | *Defiant* | 1/41 |
| 5081 *Penrice Castle* | *Lockheed Hudson* | 1/41 |
| 5082 *Powis Castle* | *Swordfish* | 1/41 |
| 7001 *Denbigh Castle* | *Sir James Milne* | 2/48 |
| 7005 *Lamphey Castle* | *Sir Edward Elgar* | 8/57 |
| 7007 *Ogmore Castle* | *Great Western* | 1/48 |

*renumbered 100 A1

*Although not used, both the *Picton Castle* nameplates were completed, but were subsequently stripped, and the backplates re-used to form new nameplates for Spitfire (No 5071).

The removal of the name and the re-use of backplates is also known to have taken place on two other occasions. During May 1946 the backplates from *Cranbrook Castle* (No 5073) were used for *Viscount Portal* (No 7000) and those from *Drysllwyn Castle* (No 5076) were used to make up *Elmley Castle* (No 7003). New nameplates were subsequently made for Nos 7018 and 7030 in 1949 and 1950 respectively.

In February 1952 the number and name of No 4082 *Windsor Castle* were transferred to engine No 7013, and the number and name No 7013 *Bristol Castle* were in turn transferred to No 4082. Both locomotives continued to run in this guise until withdrawal.

The following 'Castle' names were allocated but not used!

5007 *Oystermouth Castle*  5053 *Hatherop Castle*  7035 *Liddington Castle*
5012 *Wallingford Castle*  5058 *Picton Castle**
5027 *Exeter Castle*  5067 *Wilton Castle*

# **A**ppendix Four

## 'CASTLE' ALLOCATIONS

| No | 1929 | 1932 | 1935 | 1938 | 1941 | 1944 | 1947 | 1950 | 1954 | 1957 | 1960 | 1963 | Final | Wdn |
|---|---|---|---|---|---|---|---|---|---|---|---|---|---|---|
| 111 | PDN | PDN | PDN | PDN | PDN | PDN | PDN | LA | | | | | LA | 6/53 |
| 4000 | NA | PDN | SALOP | WSR | WSR | WSR | WSR | WSR | WSR | LDR | | | LDR | 5/57 |
| 4009 | NA | BL | PDN | PDN | PDN | PDN | PDN | PDN | | | | | PDN | 3/50 |
| 4016 | WSR | WSR | BL | BL | NA | NA | NA | NA | | | | | PDN | 9/51 |
| 4032 | NA | NA | LA | LA | LA | LA | LA | LA | | | | | TN | 9/51 |
| 4037 | PDN | PDN | PDN | PDN | PDN | PDN | PDN | PDN | PDN | NA | NA | - | EXE | 9/62 |
| 4073 | PDN | PDN | PDN | PDN | PDN | PDN | PDN | PDN | BL | CDF | CDF | | CDF | 5/60 |
| 4074 | PDN | NA | EXE | CDF | LDR | LDR | LDR | LDR | LDR | CAR | LDR | PDN | PDN | 5/63 |
| 4075 | EXE | CDF | PDN | PDN | PDN | PDN | PDN | PDN | BL | BL | PDN | | PDN | 11/61 |
| 4076 | EXE | PDN | EXE | EXE | SALOP | PDN | PDN | CHR | CHR | CHR | LDR | LLY | LLY | 2/63 |
| 4077 | PDN | CDF | NA | NA | LA | NA | NA | NA | NA | LA | NA | | BL* | 8/62 |
| 4078 | PDN | CDF | SALOP | LDR | LDR | LDR | LDR | LDR | LDR | LDR | BAN | | LLY | 7/62 |
| 4079 | PDN | BL | WSR | CDF | GLO | GLO | HFD | GLO | WSR | WSR | BL | SDN | BL* | 5/64 |
| 4080 | NA | NA | LDR | LDR | LDR | NA | BL | LDR | NA | BL | BL | CVED | SHL | 8/64 |
| 4081 | PDN | LA | BL | BL | BL | BL | LDR | SDN | LDR | LDR | SALOP | | CAR | 1/63 |
| 4082 | NA | PDN | BL | PDN | PDN | GLO | GLO | WOS | PDN | PDN | PDN | PDN | TYS | 2/65 |
| 4083 | PDN | PDN | LA | CDF | CDF | CDF | CDF | CDF | WSR | WSR | NA | | CDF | 12/61 |
| 4084 | LA | NA | PDN | BL | BL | BL | BL | BL | BL | BL | CDF | | CDF | 10/60 |
| 4085 | LA | CAR | EXE | PDN | RDG | RDG | RDG | RDG | RDG | RDG | GLO | | PDN | 5/62 |
| 4086 | LA | CAR | CDF | GLO | WOS | WOS | WOS | WOS | LA | LA | CDF | | RDG | 4/62 |
| 4087 | NA | LA | PDN | PZ | LA | LA | LA | PZ | PZ | LA | LA | LA | BL* | 10/63 |
| 4088 | NA | WSR | LA | PDN | LA | LA | LA | LA | NA | LA | WOS | SDN | BL* | 5/64 |
| 4089 | CDF | PDN | WSR | SDN | SDN | BL | BL | LA | LA | PDN | WOS | PDN | RDG | 9/64 |
| 4090 | PDN | LA | PZ | LA | LA | LA | LA | LA | WSR | SDN | CAR | CVED | CVED | 6/63 |
| 4091 | PDN | BL | CDF | CDF | PDN | PDN | PDN | LA | BL | PDN | - | | PDN | 1/59 |
| 4092 | PDN | CDF | LA | LA | WOS | WOS | WOS | WOS | WSR | WSR | RDG | | OX | 12/61 |
| 4093 | PDN | PDN | CDF | LA | LA | BL | BL | BL | LDR | LDR | LDR | LDR | GLO | 9/64 |
| 4094 | PDN | NA | LA | CDF | CDF | CDF | CDF | CDF | BL | WSR | LDR | | CDF | 3/62 |
| 4095 | NA | NA | NA | LDR | LDR | LDR | LDR | LDR | LDR | LDR | PZ | | RDG | 12/62 |
| 4096 | NA | NA | LDR | BL | BL | BL | BL | BL | BL | BL | PDN | | LLY | 1/63 |
| 4097 | PDN | CDF | BL | LA | NA | NA | PZ | EXE | PDN | PDN | LDR | | LDR | 5/60 |
| 4098 | PDN | NA | EXE | EXE | LA | NA | LA | NA | NA | NA | NA | PDN | PDN | 12/63 |
| 4099 | PDN | CDF | PDN | EXE | EXE | NA | NA | NA | NA | PZ | LDR | | LLY | 9/62 |
| 5000 | PDN | PDN | LA | PDN | PDN | PDN | PDN | PDN | BL | SDN | SDN | GLO | OXY | 10/64 |
| 5001 | PDN | PDN | WSR | PDN | CDF | CDF | CDF | CDF | CDF | PDN | SALOP | PDN | PDN | 2/63 |
| 5002 | PDN | LA | CDF | CDF | LDR | LDR | LDR | LDR | LDR | SDN | SDN | SDN | SHL | 9/64 |
| 5003 | PDN | PDN | CDF | EXE | EXE | TN | TN | TN | EXE | EXE | NA | | NA | 8/62 |
| 5004 | LA | NA | CDF | PDN | PDN | PDN | PDN | PDN | PDN | SALOP | LDR | | NEA | 4/62 |
| 5005 | PDN | LA | PDN | PDN | PDN | PDN | CDF | CDF | CDF | NA | SDN | - | SDN | 2/60 |
| 5006 | PDN | PDN | LDR | PDN | BL | LDR | LDR | CDF | CDF | PDN | CAR | | CAR | 4/62 |
| 5007 | LA | LA | PDN | WSR | CDF | CDF | CDF | CDF | CDF | PDN | SDN | | GLO | 9/62 |
| 5008 | LA | CAR | PDN | PDN | PDN | PDN | PDN | PDN | WSR | PDN | PDN | | PDN | 9/62 |
| 5009 | NA | PDN | LA | NA | LA | LA | LA | SDN | SDN | SDN | SDN | | SDN | 10/62 |
| 5010 | PDN | LA | CDF | CDF | CDF | CDF | CDF | LDR | WSR | WSR | - | | RDG | 10/59 |
| 5011 | NA | CDF | LA | NA | PZ | NA | NA | NA | NA | NA | NA | | PDN | 9/62 |
| 5012 | NA | PDN | CDF | CDF | EXE | EXE | EXE | EXE | OXF | OXF | OXF | | OXF | 4/62 |
| 5013 | - | - | EXE | LA | LDR | LDR | LDR | LDR | LDR | LDR | LDR | | NEA | 7/62 |
| 5014 | - | - | NA | PDN | BL | PDN | PDN | PDN | PDN | PDN | PDN | PDN | TYS | 2/65 |
| 5015 | - | - | EXE | LA | PDN | SALOP | WSR | WSR | WSR | WSR | BL | CVED | CVED | 4/63 |
| 5016 | - | - | NA | PZ | LDR | LDR | LDR | LDR | LDR | LDR | LDR | | LLY | 9/62 |
| 5017 | - | - | NA | NA | WOS | WOS | WOS | WOS | GLO | GLO | GLO | | GLO | 9/62 |
| 5018 | - | - | PDN | PDN | PDN | PDN | WSR | st | GLO | GLO | RDG | RDG | RDG | 3/64 |
| 5019 | - | - | NA | LA | BL | BL | BL | BL | BL | BL | WSR | | WSR | 9/62 |
| 5020 | - | - | CDF | LDR | CDF | CDF | CDF | CDF | CDF | LA | PZ | | LLY | 11/62 |
| 5021 | - | - | LA | LA | SALOP | WSR | SALOP | LA | EXE | EXE | CDF | | CDF | 9/62 |
| 5022 | - | - | PDN | PDN | PDN | PDN | PDN | WSR | WSR | WSR | WSR | WSR | WSR | 6/63 |
| 5023 | - | - | PDN | PDN | PDN | PDN | PDN | st | PZ | LA | SDN | SDN | SDN | 2/63 |

| No | 1929 | 1932 | 1935 | 1938 | 1941 | 1944 | 1947 | 1950 | 1954 | 1957 | 1960 | 1963 | Final | Wdn |
|---|---|---|---|---|---|---|---|---|---|---|---|---|---|---|
| 5024 | - | - | NA | LA | LA | BL | BL | NA | NA | NA | NA | | NA | 5/62 |
| 5025 | - | - | PDN | BL | BL | BL | BL | BL | BL | SDN | OXF | OXF | HFD | 11/63 |
| 5026 | - | - | NA | EXE | EXE | EXE | EXE | LA | OXF | OXF | WSR | WSR | OXY | 11/64 |
| 5027 | - | - | PDN | PDN | PDN | PDN | PDN | PDN | WSR | BL | PDN | | LLY | 11/62 |
| 5028 | - | - | LA | NA | NA | NA | NA | NA | NA | LA | LA | | LA | 5/60 |
| 5029 | - | - | PDN | PDN | PDN | PDN | PDN | PDN | PDN | PDN | LA | CVED | CVED | 12/63 |
| 5030 | - | - | EXE | CDF | CDF | CDF | CDF | CDF | CDF | CDF | CAR | | CAR | 9/62 |
| 5031 | - | - | WSR | WSR | WSR | WSR | WSR | WSR | WSR | WSR | WSR | WSR | WSR | 10/63 |
| 5032 | - | - | SALOP | SALOP | SALOP | SALOP | SALOP | WSR | WSR | WSR | NA | | PDN | 9/62 |
| 5033 | - | - | WSR | WSR | WSR | WSR | WSR | CHR | CHR | CHR | OXF | | OXF | 9/62 |
| 5034 | - | - | NA | NA | NA | NA | NA | NA | PDN | PDN | PDN | | PDN | 9/62 |
| 5035 | - | - | CDF | WSR | PDN | PDN | PDN | PDN | PDN | PDN | PDN | | SDN | 5/62 |
| 5036 | - | - | - | PDN | PDN | PDN | PDN | PDN | RDG | RDG | RDG | | PDN | 9/62 |
| 5037 | - | - | - | PDN | PDN | PDN | PDN | st | BL | WOS | WOS | NEA | BL* | 3/64 |
| 5038 | - | - | - | PDN | PDN | PDN | PDN | PDN | PDN | PDN | SALOP | RDG | RDG | 9/63 |
| 5039 | - | - | - | PDN | PDN | PDN | PDN | PDN | CAR | CAR | CAR | LDR | RDG | 6/64 |
| 5040 | - | - | - | PDN | PDN | PDN | PDN | PDN | PDN | PDN | PDN | BL* | BL* | 10/63 |
| 5041 | - | - | - | LA | LA | LA | LA | st | NA | LDR | LDR | PDN | PDN | 12/63 |
| 5042 | - | - | - | WOS | GLO | GLO | GLO | GLO | GLO | GLO | WOS | CAR | GLO | 6/65 |
| 5043 | - | - | - | PDN | PDN | PDN | PDN | PDN | CAR | PDN | PDN | CVED | CVED | 12/63 |
| 5044 | - | - | - | PDN | PDN | PDN | PDN | PDN | PDN | PDN | PDN | | CDF | 3/62 |
| 5045 | - | - | - | PDN | PDN | PDN | PDN | PDN | WSR | WSR | WSR | | WSR | 9/62 |
| 5046 | - | - | - | CDF | CDF | CDF | CDF | CDF | CDF | CDF | WSR | | WSR | 9/62 |
| 5047 | - | - | - | LA | NA | LA | NA | NA | NA | WSR | WSR | | WSR | 8/62 |
| 5048 | - | - | - | BL | BL | BL | BL | BL | BL | BL | BL | - | LLY | 8/62 |
| 5049 | - | - | - | WOS | CDF | CDF | CDF | CDF | CDF | LA | NA | BL* | BL* | 3/63 |
| 5050 | - | - | - | WOS | EXE | LA | LA | st | SALOP | SALOP | SALOP | BL* | BL* | 8/63 |
| 5051 | - | - | - | LDR | LDR | LDR | LDR | LDR | LDR | LDR | LDR | NEA | NEA | 5/63 |
| 5052 | - | - | - | CDF | CDF | CDF | CDF | CDF | CDF | PDN | PDN | | BL* | 9/62 |
| 5053 | - | - | - | WSR | WSR | WSR | WSR | WSR | WSR | NA | LA | | CDF | 7/62 |
| 5054 | - | - | - | PDN | CDF | CDF | CDF | CDF | CDF | CDF | PDN | NEA | GLO | 10/64 |
| 5055 | - | - | - | PDN | PDN | PDN | PDN | PDN | PDN | PDN | NA | PDN | GLO | 9/64 |
| 5056 | - | - | - | PDN | PDN | PDN | PDN | PDN | PDN | PDN | PDN | PDN | OXY | 11/64 |
| 5057 | - | - | - | NA | LA | LA | LA | LA | LA | BL | BAN | PDN | PDN | 3/64 |
| 5058 | - | - | - | NA | NA | NA | NA | NA | LA | LA | LA | GLO | GLO | 3/63 |
| 5059 | - | - | - | EXE | EXE | EXE | EXE | EXE | NA | NA | SALOP | | SALOP | 6/62 |
| 5060 | - | - | - | WSR | LA | LA | LA | LA | PDN | PDN | PDN | PDN | PDN | 4/63 |
| 5061 | - | - | - | SALOP | SALOP | SALOP | SALOP | CHR | CHR | CDF | | | CDF | 9/62 |
| 5062 | - | - | - | NA | NA | NA | NA | NA | SDN | SDN | BL | | LLY | 8/62 |
| 5063 | - | - | - | WOS | WOS | WOS | WOS | WOS | WOS | BL | WSR | WSR | OXY | 2/65 |
| 5064 | - | - | - | SALOP | SALOP | SALOP | SALOP | BL | BL | SDN | | | GLO | 9/62 |
| 5065 | - | - | - | EXE | CDF | CDF | PDN | st | PDN | PDN | PDN | | PDN | 1/63 |
| 5066 | - | - | - | PDN | PDN | PDN | PDN | st | PDN | PDN | PDN | | PDN | 9/62 |
| 5067 | - | - | - | PDN | PDN | SDN | SDN | BL | BL | BL | BL | | RDG | 7/62 |
| 5068 | - | - | - | - | BL | SDN | SDN | SDN | SDN | SDN | SDN | | OXF | 9/62 |
| 5069 | - | - | - | - | PDN | PDN | PDN | PDN | BL | LA | LA | | LA | 2/62 |
| 5070 | - | - | - | - | WSR | WSR | WSR | WSR | WSR | WSR | WSR | PDN | PDN | 3/64 |
| 5071 | - | - | - | - | NA | NA | NA | NA | NA | NA | WOS | BL* | BL* | 10/64 |
| 5072 | - | - | - | - | NA | NA | NA | LDR | LDR | LA | WSR | | WSR | 10/62 |
| 5073 | - | - | - | - | SALOP | SALOP | SALOP | SALOP | SALOP | SALOP | BL | CVED | CVED | 2/64 |
| 5074 | - | - | - | - | BL | BL | BL | BL | BL | PDN | PDN | CVED | BL* | 5/64 |
| 5075 | - | - | - | - | WSR | WSR | WSR | CHR | CHR | WSR | EXE | | BL* | 9/62 |
| 5076 | - | - | - | - | BL | BL | BL | BL | BL | BL | RDG | RDG | SHL | 9/64 |
| 5077 | - | - | - | - | TN | TN | LDR | TN | CDF | LDR | LDR | | LDR | 7/62 |
| 5078 | - | - | - | - | PZ | NA | NA | NA | NA | NA | BL | | NEA | 11/62 |
| 5079 | - | - | - | - | CDF | LDR | LA | NA | NA | NA | NA | | NA | 5/60 |
| 5080 | - | - | - | - | CDF | CDF | CDF | CDF | CDF | LDR | LDR | LLY | LLY | 4/63 |
| 5081 | - | - | - | - | WSR | WSR | PDN | PDN | PDN | WOS | WOS | CVED | CVED | 9/63 |
| 5082 | - | - | - | - | BL | BL | BL | BL | PDN | PDN | PDN | | PDN | 6/62 |
| 5083 | - | - | - | - | LDR | LDR | SDN | SDN | SDN | WOS | - | | WOS | 1/59 |
| 5084 | - | - | - | - | BL | BL | SDN | SDN | SDN | PDN | PDN | | PDN | 7/62 |
| 5085 | - | - | - | - | PDN | PDN | PDN | PDN | BL | BL | BL | NEA | BL* | 2/64 |
| 5086 | - | - | - | - | WSR | SALOP | SALOP | WOS | WOS | - | | | WOS | 11/58 |
| 5087 | - | - | - | - | PDN | PDN | PDN | PDN | PDN | PDN | PDN | LLY | LLY | 8/63 |
| 5088 | - | - | - | - | SALOP | WSR | WSR | WSR | WSR | WSR | WSR | | WSR | 9/62 |
| 5089 | - | - | - | - | LDR | LDR | LDR | CDF | CDF | LA | WSR | WSR | OXY | 11/64 |
| 5090 | - | - | - | - | LA | LA | LA | LA | WOS | WOS | BL | | PDN | 5/62 |
| 5091 | - | - | - | - | BL | BL | BL | SDN | SALOP | CHR | LDR | CVED | TYS | 10/64 |
| 5092 | - | - | - | - | WOS | WOS | WOS | WOS | WOS | PDN | BL | CVED | CVED | 7/63 |
| 5093 | - | - | - | - | LDR | LDR | LDR | LDR | PDN | PDN | PDN | PDN | PDN | 9/63 |
| 5094 | - | - | - | - | NA | NA | NA | st | BL | GLO | GLO | | BL* | 9/62 |

| No | 1929 | 1932 | 1935 | 1938 | 1941 | 1944 | 1947 | 1950 | 1954 | 1957 | 1960 | 1963 | Final | Wdn |
|---|---|---|---|---|---|---|---|---|---|---|---|---|---|---|
| 5095 | - | - | - | - | LA | LA | LA | LA | PDN | CDF | CDF | | SALOP | 8/62 |
| 5096 | - | - | - | - | BL | BL | BL | BL | BL | BL | BL | CVED | WOS | 6/64 |
| 5097 | - | - | - | - | - | SALOP | SALOP | SALOP | SALOP | SALOP | BL | CVED | CVED | 3/63 |
| 5098 | - | - | - | - | - | - | EXE | LA | LA | LA | LA | CAR | RDG | 6/64 |
| 5099 | - | - | - | - | - | - | SND | CDF | CDF | PDN | CDF | GLO | GLO | 2/63 |
| 7000 | - | - | - | - | - | - | NA | NA | NA | NA | GLO | GLO | WOS | 12/63 |
| 7001 | - | - | - | - | - | - | FDN | PDN | PDN | PDN | PD | WSR | OXY | 9/63 |
| 7002 | - | - | - | - | - | - | LDR | LDR | LDR | CAR | WOS | WOS | WOS | 3/64 |
| 7003 | - | - | - | - | - | - | LDR | LDR | LDR | LDR | BL | GLO | GLO | 8/64 |
| 7004 | - | - | - | - | - | - | GLO | PDN | PDN | PDN | PDN | WOS | RDG | 1/64 |
| 7005 | - | - | - | - | - | - | WOS | WOS | WOS | WOS | WOS | WOS | WOS | 9/64 |
| 7006 | - | - | - | - | - | - | GLO | GLO | GLO | GLO | CDF | PDN | PDN | 12/63 |
| 7007 | - | - | - | - | - | - | WOS | WOS | WOS | WOS | WOS | WOS | WOS | 2/63 |
| 7008 | - | - | - | - | - | - | - | OXF | OXF | OXF | OXF | OXF | PDN | 9/64 |
| 7009 | - | - | - | - | - | - | - | LDR | LDR | LDR | LDR | PDN | GLO | 3/63 |
| 7010 | - | - | - | - | - | - | - | OXF | PDN | PDN | PDN | PDN | RDG | 3/64 |
| 7011 | - | - | - | - | - | - | - | BL | BL | BL | BAN | RDG | OXY | 2/65 |
| 7012 | - | - | - | - | - | - | - | LDR | LDR | LDR | CAR | WSR | OXY | 11/64 |
| 7013 | - | - | - | - | - | - | - | PDN | WOS | WOS | PDN | WOS | GLO | 2/65 |
| 7014 | - | - | - | - | - | - | - | BL | BL | BL | BL | WSR | TYS | 2/65 |
| 7015 | - | - | - | - | - | - | - | SDN | SDN | BL | SALOP | PDN | PDN | 4/63 |
| 7016 | - | - | - | - | - | - | - | CDF | CDF | LDR | CAR | - | CVED | 11/62 |
| 7017 | - | - | - | - | - | - | - | CDF | CDF | PDN | PDN | PDN | PDN | 2/63 |
| 7018 | - | - | - | - | - | - | - | LDR | LDR | BL | BL | PDN | PDN | 9/63 |
| 7019 | - | - | - | - | - | - | - | BL | BL | BL | BL | WSR | OXY | 2/64 |
| 7020 | - | - | - | - | - | - | - | CDF | CDF | PDN | PDN | PDN | SHL | 9/64 |
| 7021 | - | - | - | - | - | - | - | LDR | LDR | LDR | LDR | PDN | PDN | 9/63 |
| 7022 | - | - | - | - | - | - | - | CDF | CDF | LA | LA | LA | GLO | 6/65 |
| 7023 | - | - | - | - | - | - | - | CDF | CDF | CDF | CDF | WOS | OXY | 2/65 |
| 7024 | - | - | - | - | - | - | - | PDN | PDN | PDN | PDN | WSR | OXY | 2/65 |
| 7025 | - | - | - | - | - | - | - | PDN | PDN | PDN | PDN | WOS | WOS | 9/64 |
| 7026 | - | - | - | - | - | - | - | WSR | WSR | WSR | WSR | WSR | TYS | 10/64 |
| 7027 | - | - | - | - | - | - | - | LA | PDN | PDN | PDN | WOS | RDG | 12/63 |
| 7028 | - | - | - | - | - | - | - | - | LDR | CAR | LDR | LLY | LLY | 12/63 |
| 7029 | - | - | - | - | - | - | - | - | NA | NA | NA | PDN | GLO | 12/65 |
| 7030 | - | - | - | - | - | - | - | - | PDN | PDN | PDN | PDN | PDN | 12/65 |
| 7031 | - | - | - | - | - | - | - | - | LA | LA | LA | WOS | WOS | 7/63 |
| 7032 | - | - | - | - | - | - | - | - | PDN | PDN | PDN | PDN | PDN | 9/64 |
| 7033 | - | - | - | - | - | - | - | - | PDN | PDN | PDN | PDN | PDN | 1/63 |
| 7034 | - | - | - | - | - | - | - | - | BL | BL | BL | GLO | GLO | 6/65 |
| 7035 | - | - | - | - | - | - | - | - | GLO | BL | LDR | OXF | PDN | 6/64 |
| 7036 | - | - | - | - | - | - | - | - | PDN | PDN | PDN | PDN | PDN | 9/63 |
| 7037 | - | - | - | - | - | - | - | - | SDN | SDN | SDN | PDN | SDN | 3/63 |

For continuity Great Western shed codes have been used throughout. The above allocations are from the Great Western and Western Region engine books at Kew and are correct to 1st January each year.

| CODE | SHED | BR 1950 CODE | |
|---|---|---|---|
| PDN | Old Oak Common | 81A | |
| SHL | Southall | 81C | |
| RDG | Reading | 81D | |
| OXF | Oxford | 81F | |
| BL | Bristol Bath Rd | 82A | |
| BL* | Bristol St Philips Marsh | | 82B |
| SDN | Swindon | 82C | |
| WEY | Weymouth | 82F | |
| NA | Newton Abbot | 83A | |
| TN | Taunton | 83B | |
| EXE | Exeter | 83C | |
| LA | Plymouth Laira | 83D | |
| PZ | Penzance | 83G | |

| CODE | SHED | BR 1950 CODE | |
|---|---|---|---|
| WSR | Wolverhampton Stafford Rd | 84A | |
| OXY | Wolverhampton Oxley | | 84B |
| BAN | Banbury | 84C | |
| TYS | Tyseley | 84E | |
| SALOP | Shrewsbury | | 84G |
| CHR | Chester | 84K | |
| WOS | Worcester | 85A | |
| GLO | Gloucester | 85B | |
| HFD | Hereford | 85C | |
| CDF | Cardiff Canton | | 86C |
| NEA | Neath | 87A | |
| LDR | Llandore | 87E | |

# Appendix Five

## 'CASTLE' CLASS LIVERIES

All 'Castles' constructed during Great Western days were turned out from new in Collett's express passenger livery of 'middle chrome green'. Smokeboxes, underframes, and wheels were in black. The green was finished off with an orange and black lining. The only exceptions came during 1932 when No 4089 was painted in a lighter shade of green and again during World War 2 when Nos 5001/18 were turned out in wartime unlined black.

In 1948 the newly formed Western Region painted four engines of the 1948 batch, Nos 7010/11/12/13, in an experimental light apple green livery, finished off with red and grey lining. During the same year a further five 'Castles', Nos 4089/91, 5010/21/23 were also repainted in the experimental livery. Some of these engines were fitted with brass smokebox numberplates. The apple green was not a success and was eventually removed. Swindon continued to turn out its 'Castles' in Great Western green, a colour that was eventually adopted by the British Railways Board as the standard livery for all of its express passenger locomotives!

*Below:*
**No 7011 *Banbury Castle* in experimental apple green livery and with a brass smokebox numberplate stands at Bristol Temple Meads c1948.** *Real Photos*

# Appendix Six

## PRINCIPAL DIMENSIONS OF 'CASTLE' CLASS

*Below:*
**Diagram showing general layout of 'Castle' class.** *Ian Allan Library*

*Bottom:*
**Diagram showing four-row superheater and double blastpipe arrangement as fitted to 'Castle' class locomotives.**
*Ian Allan Library*

|  | *Original* | *4-row Superheater* |
|---|---|---|
| Boiler Pressure: | 225lb/sq. in. | 225lb/sq in |
| Cylinders (four): | 16inx26in | 16inx26in |
| Wheel diameter: | 6ft 8½in | 6ft 8½in |
| Tractive Effort, pressure: 85% | 31,625lb | 31,625lb |
| Evap heating surface: | 2,049sq ft | 1,833sq ft |
| Grate Area: | 30.3sq ft | 29.4sq ft |
| Superheating surface: | 262.6sq ft | 380sq ft |
| Max axle load: | 19.7tons | 20tons |
| Adhesion weight: | 58.85 tons | 59.5 tons |
| Engine weight working order: | 79.85 tons | 80.75 tons |
| Coupled wheelbase: | 14ft.9in | 14ft.9in |
| Engine wheelbase: | 27ft.3in | 27ft.3in |
| Tender water: | 3,500gals | 4,000 tons |
| Engine + Tender capacity weight: | 119.85 tons | 129.75 tons |
| Total length engine + tender: | 65ft 2in | 65ft 2in |
| Height from rail level ft/in: | 13ft.5½in | 13ft 0¾in |

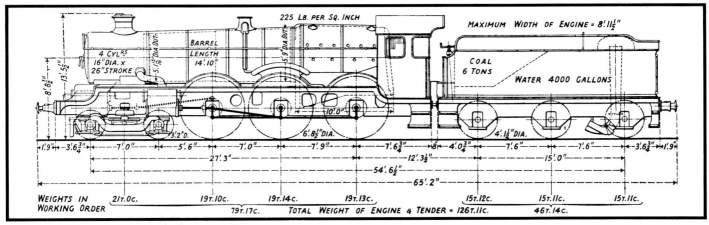

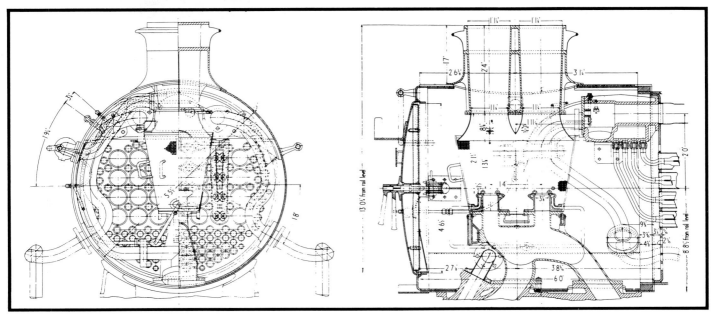

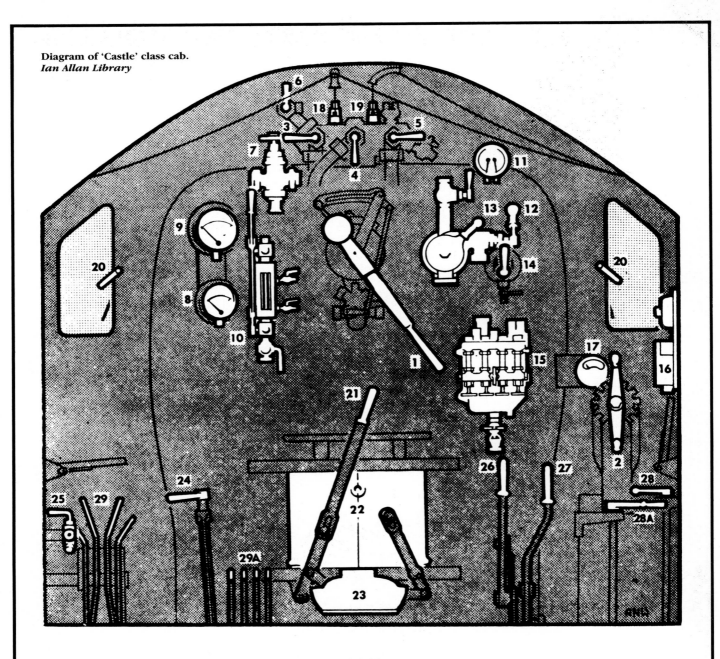

**Diagram of 'Castle' class cab.**
*Ian Allan Library*

## KEY

1. Regulator handle.
2. Reversing gear handle.
3. Exhaust injector live steam valve.
4. Exhaust steam injector auxiliary steam valve.
5. Right-hand injector live steam valve.
6. Steam heating valve.
7. Steam heating pressure regulator.
8. Steam heating pressure gauge.
9. Boiler steam pressure gauge.
10. Water level gauge.
11. Duplex vacuum brake gauge.
12. Ejector steam valve.
13. Brake application lever.
14. Blower valve.
15. Hydrostatic lubricator

16. Audible signalling and automatic train control apparatus.
17. Speedometer.
18. Signal whistle valve.
19. Brake whistle valve.
20. Screen wipers
21. Firedoor operating lever.
22. Double fire-doors.
23. Firehole half door.
24. Exhaust injector water regulator.
25. Coal watering cock.
26. Cylinder cocks control lever.
27. Front sanding lever.
28. Rear sanding lever.
28a. Rear sanding lever alternative position.
29. Air damper levers.
29a. Air damper levers alternative position.

# Appendix Seven

## 'CASTLES' IN PRESERVATION

| No | Name | Present Location | Status |
|----|------|------------------|--------|
| 4073 | *Caerphilly Castle* | Science Museum London | S/E |
| 4079 | *Pendennis Castle* | Hammersley Australia | R/O |
| 5029 | *Nunney Castle* | Didcot Railway Centre | R/O |
| 5043 | *Earl of Mount Edgcumbe* | Tyseley | N/O |
| 5051 | *Earl Bathurst\** | Didcot Railway Centre | N/O |
| 5080 | *Defiant* | Toddington | R/O |
| 7027 | *Thornbury Castle* | Buckfastleigh | N/O |
| 7029 | *Clun Castle* | Tyseley | R/O |

*Below:*
**The 'Western Stalwart' railtour, doubleheaded by Nos 7029 *Clun Castle* and 4930 *Hagley Hall* approaches Pontypool Road with the return working from Newport to Shrewsbury in July 1985.** *A. Doyle*

*Overleaf:*
**Highly polished, silver-buffered and unidentified, a 'Castle' swings into Newport with the 2.30pm Neyland-Paddington express.** *Ian Allan Library*

R/O Running Order,
N/O Not Operational
S/E Static Exhibit
*restored but not currently operational